The Book of Ruth

Historical and Prophetic Truths

Don T. Phillips

"The Book of Ruth: Historical and Prophetic Truths," by Don T. Phillips. ISBN 978-1-62137-825-9 (Hardcover).

Published 2016 by Virtualbookworm.com Publishing, Inc., P.O. Box 9949, College Station, TX 77842, US.

The following books are also available from Don T. Phillips:

The Book of Revelation: Mysteries Revealed

The Book of Exodus: Historical and Prophetic Truths

The Birth and Death of Christ

A Biblical Chronology from Adam to Christ

All are available from:

Virtual Bookworm Publishing Company, PO Box 9949, College Station Texas, 77842

www.virtualbookworm.com

Dedication

I would like to dedicate this book to five people who have played a special role in my religious maturity in Jesus Christ.

Dr. Terry Teykle .... A Man of Prayer

Dr. Bruce Wood.........A Mentor and Role Model

Dr. Robert Johnson..... A Man of Faith and Covenant
Keeper

Pastor Dan Cummins... A Biblical Scholar and Teacher of
the Word

And.........

Candyce J. Phillips.......Lifelong Companion and a
Woman of Faith

Earth's saddest day and
gladdest day were just...

three days apart.

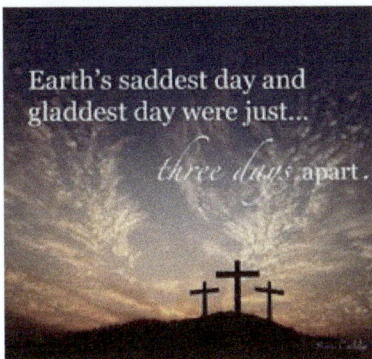

Table of Contents

[37] *Then saith He unto his disciples, the harvest truly is plenteous, but the laborers are few;*
[38] *Pray ye therefore the Lord of the harvest, that he will send forth laborers into his harvest.* Matthew 9:37-38

Preface

The first time that I heard Ruth taught from the pulpit was in 1984 by Pastor Dan Cummins; a pastor, mentor, friend and biblical scholar. I can remember that the Book of Ruth was presented as a classical Jewish story of love, devotion and faith by a Gentile woman from Moab who converted to the Jewish faith. The story was interesting but I can remember that it impressed me as a historical account of how a Gentile woman became a Jewish proselyte; the name given by the Jews to foreigners who adopted the Jewish religion. An interesting message to me at that time was how a man of Israel named Boaz became a kinsman redeemer for both Ruth and her mother in law Naomi, saving both from a life of poverty and despair.

As the presentation unfolded, I became intrigued by the prophetic truths imbedded in the basic story. As time passed, I found myself drawn to the Book of Ruth and the hidden (to the Jewish community) message that the Nation of Israel would be *blinded in part* and fail to recognize Jesus Christ as their long awaited messiah until the *fullness of the Gentiles would come in*. In the fullness of God's time the Children of Israel would have the *scales removed from their eyes* and recognize Jesus Christ as their own *kinsman redeemer*...... and so all of *Israel will be saved*.

i

The story of Ruth contains important information about Jewish Customs of the time, and how land and possessions were to be perpetually passed down from generation to generation. As the Book of Ruth was intently studied and revealed through the work of the Holy Spirit, deeper prophetic truths in the Book of Ruth began to be unveiled. This book will attempt to accomplish two things: (1) Interpret and analyze the story of Ruth as written by a holy scribe verse by verse (Authorized King James Version) and (2) Attempt to fully explain and present the prophetic structure of the book.

The contents of this book have been taught in several bible studies over the course of the years, and expounded and expanded as the Holy Spirit granted me license to do so. It is hoped that this study will deepen your understanding of the historical narrative, and reveal prophetic truths not previously addressed in other classical books. It must be confessed that I do not claim to have full understanding of this great book, but perhaps the explanations and discussions contained herein will open the full body of scriptural truth to all who seek His wisdom and knowledge.

I fully admit that hundreds of hours were spent reading expositions and narratives from men and women of God who were also moved to address this great book. I have collected wisdom and truth from many, many sources over a long period of time; and in my personal notes I have failed to record or remember all sources. I ask those who might recognize their wisdom to please let me know so that I can give them full credit in a future edition as I learn and mature in Christ. I am told that the greatest act of flattery is in having someone act and understand as you do. Let it be so; God knows the individuals and their contributions.

May God richly bless you as you study His Holy Word and pray for our Jewish brothers and sisters that they might turn to Jesus Christ as their redeemer and savior.

The Book of Ruth

BIBLICAL AND PROPHETIC TRUTHS

Part 1: The Story of Ruth

Introduction

The Book of Ruth is the eighth book of the Old Testament in the authorized King James Bible. It tells of how a man from Bethlehem called *Elimelech* left his land during a famine and went to the Land of Moab with his wife *Naomi* and his two sons: *Mahlon* and *Chilion*. Her sons marry Moabite women: one named *Orpah,* and the other named Ruth. Within a 10-year period of time, both Mahlon and

Chilion die, leaving both Ruth and Orpah childless widows. With no means of support, Naomi, Ruth and Orpah leave Moab for Bethlehem. On the way, Orpah turns back to Moab but Ruth decides to stay with Naomi. With Naomi's assistance, Ruth marries an older kinsman called *Boaz* who lives in the town of Bethlehem, thereby preserving her deceased husband's posterity and becoming an ancestor of King David. The story is primarily concerned with how Naomi is saved from a life of poverty and disgrace, and how Ruth is rescued by Boaz, who is a *kinsman redeemer*.

The narrative is poetically-constructed and tells a classic story of how God in His mercy turns ordinary events into extraordinary blessings. The story introduces an ancient Jewish custom concerning marriage of a family widow, called the *Leverite Law*. The story is revered by Jewish people, and is generally-recognized as containing important historical facts and prophetic truths. The Book of Ruth was originally a part of the Book of Judges, but it now forms one of the twenty-four separate books of the Hebrew Bible and is the 8th book in the Authorized King James Bible. It is composed of 4 chapters, 85 verses and 2,578 words.

According to Jewish tradition, the author of this book was probably Samuel. Although the Book of Ruth is not very long, it is remarkably rich in examples of cultural practices, faith, kindness and redemption. We will also see that it is also a book rich in prophecy, which in shadow and type reveals how Jesus Christ will ultimately redeem both Jews and Gentiles from sin and despair.

Historical Background

Now it came to pass in the days when the judges ruled...
Ruth 1:1(a)

There is no reason to assume that the Book of Ruth was in any way a fictional account. It stands as a great story of how God is faithful and merciful to those who will follow after Him and obey His holy commandments. Although the Jewish perspective of the Book of Ruth is simply to provide a glimpse into the life of ordinary people, it is to the New-Testament believer much more than that. The story of Ruth is pregnant with prophetic truths, and it provides a rare glimpse for biblical scholars and practitioners of how the coming Messiah, Jesus Christ, would use the Gentiles to bring salvation to the nation of Israel.

The setting for this magnificent story is clearly identified as a time *when the judges ruled.* The period in which judges ruled over Israel was a dark period of time in which the Nation of Israel turned to idol worship, intermarried with forbidden women, and turned their back on God. Following the Exodus from Egypt (Spring, 1490 BC-Spring,1450 BC), Israel was ruled by Joshua for a short period of time (25 years) until he died. Following his death, the elders ruled for another short period of time (20 years). The elders of Israel gave way to what has been called the *Period of the Judges.* The reign of Judges over Israel began with Othniel and ended with Samuel (379 years). It was during this period of time that the story of Ruth took place.

The Holy Scripture tells us in three different places that: *In those days, there was no King in Israel: Every man did that which was right in his own eyes* (Judges 18:1, 19:1 and 21:25). This period of time should have been one of great prosperity and peace for Israel, but they were constantly oppressed by the Assyrians, the Moabites, the Canaanites and the Ammonites. The judges ruled by divine appointment but this was a period of *theocracy*; God was the autocratic ruler over all the people and he ruled through the Judges. The Judges did not rule through one location, but they were like the old American west circuit riders; they travelled from town to town administering justice and presiding over important decisions. In an incredible act of disobedience and rebellion, the children of Israel rejected God as their sovereign King and sought to *do what was right in their own eyes.*

The apostasy and rebellion came to a head during the judgeship of Samuel. The people declared; *Give us a King like every other nation* (I Sam 8:6). Saul was chosen as King but he would not be a godly King. In a state of great remorse, Samuel declared *because you have rejected the word of the Lord, He has also rejected you* (I Sam 15:23). The Kingdom of Israel would now be ruled by *David.*

The story of Ruth actually *took place* between *when the Judges ruled* (Ruth 1:1) and the birth of a son called *Obed* (Ruth 4:27). Obed sired a son called *Jessie*, who was the father of *King David*. This places the story of Ruth likely somewhere near 1098 BC. The interested reader can read the details of this chronology in Phillips (1).

Although the events of Ruth can be determined with reasonable accuracy, it was not *written* until much later since Ruth 4:27 records the birth of David. This strongly suggests that the Book of Ruth might have been written during the reign of King David sometime between 1055-1015 BC. The author is unknown, but it has long been believed by Jewish historians that Samuel wrote the Book of Ruth. If written any later than 1016 BC, the genealogy of Ruth 4:27 would have undoubtedly included Solomon, who was the son of King David and the last King of the United Kingdom of Israel.

The Book of Ruth is short, containing only 4 chapters. Although it is not very long, we will see that it is worthy of intense investigation and provides many shadows and types of how the Jews would one day be brought back into a covenant relationship with God by Jesus Christ. It is also a book of prophecy that could not be fully understood until after the 3.5 year ministry of Jesus Christ.

The Book of Ruth is divided into six main sections:

- **The Famine and Family of Ruth** (Ruth 1:1-5)
- **The Resolve and Return of Ruth** (Ruth 1:6-22)
- **The Ancestral Rights of Ruth** (Ruth 2:1-23)
- **The Requests of Ruth** (Ruth 3:1-18)
- **The Redemption of Ruth** (Ruth 4:1-12)
- **The Lineage and Legacy of Ruth** (Ruth 4:13-22)

The Famine and Family of Ruth

Now it came to pass in the days when the judges ruled, that there was a famine in the land. And a certain man of

Bethlehem in Judah went to sojourn in the country of Moab, he, and his wife, and his two sons. Ruth 1:1

Sometime during the reign of the Judges, the people of Judah and particularly the inhabitants of Bethlehem were stricken with a great *famine*. In the Holy Scriptures the word famine is used in several different contexts. A famine could be caused by lack of rain, destructive hail storms, insect infestations and a scarcity of food during a long siege. This is the only place in the Holy Scriptures that this particular famine is mentioned, but it must have been long and severe. According to the Jewish Targum, this was one of ten famines (or calamities) which came from God to chastise his people:

> *"God has decreed ten grievous famines to take place in the world, to punish the inhabitants of the earth, before the coming of Messiah the king. The first (was) in the days of Adam; the second in the days of Lamech; the third in the days of Abraham; the fourth in the days of Isaac; the fifth in the days of Jacob;* **the sixth in the days of Boaz**; *the seventh in the days of David; the eighth in the days of Elijah the prophet; the ninth (was) in the days of Elisha in Samaria; and the tenth is yet to come. It will not be a famine of bread or of water, but of hearing a word of prophecy from the mouth of the Lord; and even now this (last) famine is grievous in the land of Israel."* http://www.heraldmag.org

We are not told what type of famine actually struck the family of Ruth but it was severe enough to cause Ruth, her husband and their two sons to leave their land and home somewhere near Bethlehem (Ruth 1:1). Recall that a severe famine had once before afflicted the Land of Canaan in the time of Jacob. It was so severe that Jacob moved his entire family to Egypt where he sought refuge. The famine of Ruth 1:1 was evidently just as severe, because otherwise Elimelech would never have left his inheritance in Judea with his wife Naomi and their two sons and journey to the *Land of Moab*. The Land of Moab was the home of the *Moabites*. This land was south and east of Jerusalem across from the Dead Sea, and it stretched from the Kingdom of Ammon in the north to the Kingdom of Edom in the south.

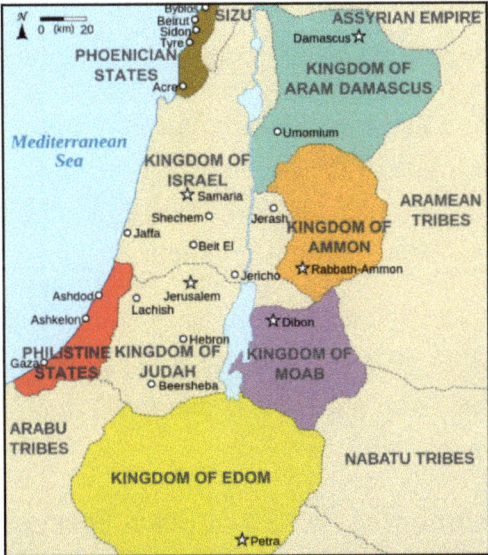

The City of Bethlehem was very near Jerusalem which was not only the capital city of Israel, but it was a center of trade and commerce. The inhabitants of the lands around Jerusalem and Bethlehem grew wheat and barley, and maintained large herds of cattle and sheep. The name *Bethlehem* might have been prophetic in two different ways. First, Bethlehem means *House of Bread* in the Hebrew language. If the famine was a severe drought that occurred over a sufficiently long period of time, the wheat and barley crops would fail due to the lack of the former (Sept/Oct) and latter rains (March/April). There would be no grain to make bread. If the barley and wheat crops failed for lack of rain, there would also be neither food nor water for both the people and their herds or flocks.

Note that the *latter and former rains* is a prophetic shadow and type of the eventual appearance of our Lord and Savior Jesus Christ, who would emerge over 1000 years later as their long-awaited Messiah.

*Then shall we know, if we follow on to know the LORD: his going forth is prepared as the morning; and he shall come unto us as the **rain**, as the **latter** and **former** rain unto the earth.* Hoshea 6:3

During His 3.5-year earthly ministry, Christ used the symbolism of *bread* to describe his character and purpose.

*Our fathers did eat manna in the desert; as it is written, He gave them **bread from heaven** to eat. Then Jesus said unto them, Verily, verily, I say unto you, Moses gave you not that **bread** from heaven; but my Father giveth you the true **bread** from heaven. For the **bread** of God is he which cometh down from heaven, and giveth life unto the world. Then said they unto him, Lord, evermore give us this **bread**. And Jesus said unto them, **I am the bread of life**: he that cometh to me shall never hunger; and he that believeth on me shall never thirst.* John 6:31-35

Although not conclusive, we can assume that by the basic entomology of the word *famine*, the meaning of Bethlehem, and the prophetic linkage to the very words of Jesus Christ that this *famine* was an extended drought in which there was no bread to eat. It is also implied that this drought in Bethlehem was common to much of Israel (*there was a famine in the land*), but this is only supposition. In any case, the *famine* drove *a certain man* (Elimelech) to leave

Bethlehem with his wife (Naomi) and their two sons (Mahlon and Chilion).

The fact that Elimelech left Jerusalem because of a famine only touches the surface of what this departure actually meant. Elimelech was an Israelite, and each male Israelite had certain privileges under the law which were both unique and interesting. Any property (house or field) owned by a male Israelite was to be perpetually passed down from father to son. This was to be an inheritance from generation to generation. In the master plan of God, property was never intended to be sold or transferred out of the tribe of Israel to which it was given when Joshua distributed the land.

The Land of Canaan was distributed by Joshua to each tribe after a 7-year conquest of the land. Within each tribe, every family was given an inheritance. It is interesting that the land never actually belonged to each Israelite; it belonged to God. The children of Israel were only *temporary residents* of the land.

*The land shall not be sold for ever: for **the land is mine;** for ye are strangers and sojourners with me.*
Leviticus 25:23

The Land of Promise was given as a perpetual, unconditional inheritance to the Tribes of Israel but this does not imply that the Israelites would prosper in the land if they were disobedient to God's word. It is also a historical fact that the land promised to Israel through Abraham was never fully conquered or dwelt upon by the children of Israel. The ultimate fulfillment of God's promises will not occur until the 1000 year Millennial Kingdom. This is because of disobedience and lack of faith.

For ye shall pass over Jordan to go in to possess the land which the LORD your God giveth you, and ye shall possess it, and dwell therein. And ye shall observe to do all the statutes and judgments which I set before you this day.
Deuteronomy 11: 31-32

Keep his decrees and commands, which I am giving you today, so that it may go well with you and your children after you and that you may live long in the land the Lord your God gives you for all time.   Deuteronomy 4:40

Possession of the Promised Land is *unconditional*, but prosperity, safety and the protection of the children of Israel that live in the land is *conditional*. It is a terrible tragedy when man deliberately and willfully beaks any covenant relationship which God has placed before him. The land had been promised to Israel and the people would prosper as long as they obeyed the Lord and trusted in His word. Elimelech clearly lacked the faith to trust in God to deliver him and his family. Although we can criticize Elimelech for his actions, is it so difficult to believe? How many times have Christians today blamed God for trials and tribulations that are experienced? Have we not read and understood the words of the Apostle Paul?

...confirming the souls of the disciples, and exhorting them to continue in the faith, and that we must through much **tribulation** *enter into the kingdom of God.*   Acts 14:22

...we glory in tribulations also: knowing that tribulation worketh patience; and patience, experience; and experience, hope.   Romans 5:3-4

Recall that the name Elimelech means *my God is King*. Like many people today who claim that they are Christians but cannot be recognized as one, Elimelech supposedly worshipped and recognized Jehovah God, but his actions spoke otherwise. The continued prosperity of each Israelite was conditioned upon how well they obeyed and trusted God.

If I shut up heaven that there be no rain, or if I command the locusts to devour the land, or if I send pestilence among my people; If my people, which are called by my name, shall humble themselves, and pray, and seek my face, and turn from their wicked ways; then will I hear from heaven, and will forgive their sin, and will heal their land.
II Chronicles 7:13-14

Although Elimelech left Israel to seek refuge in Moab, it was possible for him to retain his land of inheritance. He was perfectly within his rights to either lease or sell the land to another Israelite, and still have the inheritance remain in his family forever. In Ruth 4:3 we are told that he *sold* the land to another Israelite. If the land was sold, how could Elimelech still retain possession of the land?

It is important to understand that the land given to the tribes of Israel were never intended to permanently leave the tribe to which it was assigned. Whether leased or sold, the land *could* be reclaimed by the original landowner. All land reverted back to the original owner during the *Year of Jubilee*. If the land was either *leased* or *sold*, it could be redeemed by the original landowner by prorating the worth of the land based upon how close the current calendar year was from the next *Year of Jubilee*. In other words, land leased or sold would revert to its original owner every 50 years.

[11] *A Jubilee shall that fiftieth year be unto you: ye shall not sow, neither reap that which groweth of itself in it, nor gather the grapes in it of thy vine undressed.*

11

[12] *For it is the jubilee; it shall be holy unto you: ye shall eat the increase thereof out of the field.*
[13] In the year of this jubilee ye shall return every man unto his possession.
[14] And if thou sell ought unto thy neighbour, or buyest ought of thy neighbor's hand, ye shall not oppress one another:
[15] According to the number of years after the jubilee thou shalt buy of thy neighbor, and according unto the number of years of the fruits he shall sell unto thee:
[16] According to the multitude of years thou shalt increase the price thereof, and according to the fewness of years thou shalt diminish the price of it: for according to the number of the years of the fruits doth he sell unto thee.
[17] Ye shall not therefore oppress one another; but thou shalt fear thy God: for I am the LORD your God.
Leviticus 25:11-17

This will later play a major role in how Naomi and Ruth were rescued by a *kinsman redeemer.*

We will shortly see that Elimelech perished in the Land of Moab and so did his two sons. The tragedy of *Elimelech* was prophetic of what was yet to be extracted upon the entire *Nation of Israel.* King Solomon was an antitype of Elimelech. King David died and left the United Kingdom of Israel in the hands of his son Solomon. Solomon started as a wise and righteous king, but he soon sunk into the depths of apostasy and adultery. Upon his death, the United Kingdom of Israel split into two parts: the Northern Kingdom (an antitype of Mahlon), and the Southern Kingdom (an antitype of Chilion). As time went by, both followed after foreign gods and worshipped idols. They both abandoned the Laws of Moses and all of Israel fell into a divided, rebellious and apostate nation. Finally, God could take no more. Although He would never completely abandon His chosen people, He allowed the Northern Kingdom to be completely destroyed by the Assyrians in 932 BC. It would not take the Southern Kingdom of Judah much longer to also feel the Wrath of God. In 586 BC, the city of Jerusalem and the Southern Kingdom of Judah fell to the Babylonian Empire, and by 605 BC the entire Nation of Israel had been taken into captivity and Solomon's Temple completely ransacked and destroyed. It was at this time that the furniture and artifacts found in the Temple were either destroyed or removed to Babylon, and the Holy Ark of the Covenant completely disappeared. Jewish writings assert that at the end of the age, the Ark of the Covenant and a new Millennial Temple will be restored to the Promised Land.

The Land of Moab

The cities of Sodom and Gomorrah were an example of what can happen to a city or a nation that turns its back on God. Sodom and Gomorrah were completely destroyed by God because of sexual immorality and complete disobedience to His commands. Recall that Lot, his wife, and his two daughters were told to flee the city before it was destroyed and not look back. As they fled, the fire and brimstone rained down upon the city. Lot's wife looked back and was turned into a pillar of salt! Lot and his two daughters continued on and rested in a cave in the Mountains of Zoar. That night a terrible thing happened. His two daughters got Lot drunk and *lay with him* so that they could bear a male child. A male child was needed to inherit the promises to Lot. The oldest daughter conceived and birthed a son called *Moab*. Moab was not a child of promise, but a child born of an incestuous act. The youngest daughter also conceived, and bore a son called

13

Ben-ammi. When Moab became an adult, he travelled south and settled in what is now called the *Land of Moab*. This land is south and east of Jerusalem, directly east of the Dead Sea and bounded by the Arnon River on the north and the Zered River on the south. Moab was the progenitor of every Moabite in that land. It was to this land that Elimelech moved his family.

Even though Moab was born out of an unnatural act of passion, the law had not yet been given when this occurred, and there was no written commandment against this incestuous act. Although God was likely very displeased, His mercy is everlasting and in an incredible act of forgiveness He actually blessed Moab and the land he inhabited. As Moses marched toward the Land of Promise, he encountered the Moabites.

And the LORD said unto me, Distress not the Moabites, neither contend with them in battle: for I will not give thee of their land for a possession; because I have given Ar unto the children of Lot for a possession.

Deuteronomy 29:9

The Moabites lived in an area which was rich and fertile. The land consisted of high, rolling plains with an abundance of water. The choice of Moab as a new place to seek refuge would have been a good one from an agricultural viewpoint. The high, cool plains of Moab would have been ideal to grow wheat and barley, and it must have been spared from the drought which devastated the inhabitants of Jerusalem (Ruth 1:22, 2:1-3).

However, after Joshua crossed the River Jordan and camped near Jericho, the Moabites were cursed by God for a serious offense against Israel. It happened as follows. After almost 40 years of wandering in the wilderness, Moses was ready to leave Kadesh-barnea and enter into the Promised Land. With God's blessing, Moses conquered any enemy put into his path by divine appointment. He marched north from Kadesh-barnea on a route east of the Dead Sea. He conquered the Canaanites and the Amorites, and then finally set camp north and west of the land of Moab. Here the story of Balam and Balak unfolds. Balaam was the son of Beor. Balaam was a prophet from Penthor on the Euphrates River, and Balak the son of Zippor was a King of Moab.

Balak had observed how Moses and Israel had conquered the Amorites and realized that Moab could be in real danger. Rather than mount a military campaign against Israel, Balak sent for Balaam to pronounce a curse upon the children of Israel. We will not describe subsequent events in any detail (it can be read in Numbers 22-24) but a quick overview is needed. Balaam was an idol worshipper and a prophet, but he knew about the powerful God of Israel. He sought instructions from God as to how to proceed, and God responded. Balaam was initially told that he could not go to Moab, but after a time God told Balaam that he could go to Balak but that he was to say nothing except what God instructed him to say. At this point Balaam departed Mesopotamia and the strange story of a talking donkey is told (Numbers 22). Balaam arrives in Moab, but refuses to curse Israel. Balak entices Balaam with more and more money until Balaam finally hatches a plan that would benefit both he and Balak.

Balaam spoke to King Balak and explained how he was unable to curse the Israelites because God had forbid him to do so. He then explained to the king how he could get the Israelites to curse themselves, thereby invoking the anger of God upon Israel. He counseled King Balak and his people to ensnare God's chosen people by offering prostitutes and unclean food sacrificed to idols. Balaam responded by inviting the men of Israel to a great feast at Shittim near where Moses was camped. Numbers 25:1-9 describes how Israel ate forbidden food, engaged in sexual immorality with the women of Moab and worshipped foreign idols. The men of Israel continued to commit whoredom with the women of Moab, worshipped the heathen god called Baal-peor and ate forbidden food. God was so incensed that he commanded Moses to kill every man that participated and to hang their heads before the Lord in the sun. A man of Israel suddenly appeared in front of Moses with a Midionite woman, and Phinehas the high priest ran them both through in the man's tent with a javelin. This pleased God and he removed his curse upon the people, but not before 24,000 men of Israel were killed.

This incident would be long-remembered by the children of Israel. It was mentioned by Joshua in Joshua 22, King David in Psalms 106, and Hosea in Hosea 9. Over 1500 years later, the Apostle John recorded in Revelation 2:14 that Balaam *taught Balak to cast a stumbling block before the children of Israel*. It is difficult to imagine the devastation and grief that Balaam brought upon Israel, and it is even more difficult to understand why Elimelech would even consider moving his family to the land of Edom. The implications of what Elimelech is about to do are further emphasized by the Lord's command to Israel.

Thou shalt not seek their peace nor their prosperity all thy days for ever.   Deuteronomy 23:6

These events have been presented to set the stage for what is about to happen to Elimelech when he arrives in Edom. We will see that the *wages of sin are death*, and that within 10 years Elimelech and his two sons would all be dead and his family left destitute.

The Departure of Elimelech

[1] *And a certain man of Bethlehem in Judah went to sojourn in the country of Moab, he, and his wife, and his two sons.*
[2] *And the name of the man was Elimelech, and the name of his wife Naomi, and the name of his two sons Mahlon and Chilion, Ephrathites of Bethlehemjudah. And they came into the country of Moab, and continued there.*
Ruth 1:1-2

The patriarch of the family that left Jerusalem was a man named *Elimelech*. He was married to a woman called *Naomi* and he had two sons; *Mahlon and Chilion*. The Greek word for *sojourn* means to visit temporarily. It is implied that Elimelech only intended to live in Moab until the severe drought was past. However, this sojourn lasted much longer (Ruth 1:4) for *they continued there* for over 10 years.

In the Old Testament, biblical figures had only a single name, and it was prophetic of the person to which it was given. The following meanings of several names will prove to be informative as we discuss the Book of Ruth.

- **Elimelech…..** *"my God is King"*
- **Naomi………** *"pleasant, lovely"*

- **Mahlon**….. *"puny and frail"*
- **Chilion**….. *"pining, introspective"*
- **Orpah**….. *"to turn away"*
- **Ruth**….. *"friend or companion"*
- **Boaz**….. *"strength and comfort"*
- **Obed**….. *"to serve"*

We will shortly see that the meaning of these names is consistent with the role that each will play in the story of Ruth.

The Death of Elimelech

[3] And Elimelech Naomi's husband died; and she was left, and her two sons.
[4] And they took them wives of the women of Moab; the name of the one was Orpah, and the name of the other Ruth: and they dwelled there about ten years. Ruth 1:3-4

We will now clarify the Jewish rules of inheritance by quoting from the Jewish Encyclopedia (Jacobs and Greenstone).

> *Among the **early Hebrews**, as well as among many other nations of antiquity, custom decided that the next of kin should enter upon the possession of the estate of a deceased person. The first-born son usually assumed the headship of the family, and succeeded to the control of the family property. When there were no sons, the dying man would appoint a trusted friend as his heir, sometimes to the exclusion of a near relative.*

It appears that from the earliest times, the Jewish Rabbis allowed a dying family patriarch to name a trusted friend to inherit the family holdings. But this basic rule did not cover all contingences. Suppose that the man died suddenly without naming anyone an heir, and also had no siblings.

18

By the time of Ruth the rules of inheritance were more comprehensive (Numbers 27, 36).

If a man die, and have no son, then ye shall cause his inheritance to pass unto his daughter. And if he have no daughter, then ye shall give his inheritance unto his brethren. And if he have no brethren, then ye shall give his inheritance unto his father's brethren. And if his father have no brethren, then ye shall give his inheritance unto his kinsman that is next to him of his family, and he shall possess it. Numbers 27:8-11

Evidently, Elimelech died not long after arriving in Moab. and left Naomi, Mahlon and Chilion to fend for themselves. The oldest son was Mahlon, It appears that that the two sons almost immediately sought wives to gain social status and possibly be given a wedding dowry. In any case, both Mahlon and Chilion took Moabite wives and settled down in the Land of Moab. The two wives were *Orpah and Ruth*. We are told in Ruth 4:7 that Ruth married Mahlon and Orpah married Chilion. However, tragedy now struck the family of Naomi. In less than ten years after they had left the Promised Land, both Mahlon and Chilion died in Moab. By the Law of Moses, the family estate would pass to any surviving daughter, but both Mahlon and Chilion had no children. The family estate must then pass to Elemilech's oldest brother… but he evidently had no brother. The heir apparent was then the nearest kinsman, and any kinsman would be in Israel, not Moab!

The Death of Mahlon and Chilion

[5] And Mahlon and Chilion died also both of them; and the woman was left of her two sons and her husband.
Ruth 1:5

19

The phrase *the woman was left of her two sons and her husband* is a poor translation, and means she was *left without her two sons and husband.* So, Naomi found herself in a desperate situation. As previously described, in ancient times if there were no male children the family holdings were passed to his daughters, who must marry another tribe member. If a man and his married sons all died without daughters, the case becomes complicated but defined by Levitical laws. The family holdings were not passed down to the man's wife or to her sons' widows; it was passed on to the dead man's *brethren,* and if this fails to *his nearest kinsman.* The land which Elimelech abandoned near Jerusalem had been leased out, and Naomi had no crops, flocks or herds to sustain her in Moab. In addition, unmarried women did not have the privileges of any family male; Moabite men did not like to deal with women in matters of state or otherwise.

Now, Naomi, Orpah and Ruth were all in a very bad situation. Ruth and Orpah had no children and no males in the immediate family. Even worse, Naomi was left "high and dry" because she was a foreigner (Israelite) residing in Moab. The inheritance of Elimelech had already passed to her oldest son who was now dead. We know that this was Chilion and that he was the husband of Ruth. From Numbers 27, there was no male in the family of Ruth to inherit the estate of Elimelech. We will now repeat and simplify the rules of inheritance at the time that the Book of Ruth took place.

Rules of Inheritance

If the patriarch (father) died, the following rules applied according to the Torah, Leviticus 25 and Numbers 27.
- If the wife (widow) had sons, the estate would pass to the oldest living son.

- If the wife had no sons and only daughters, the estate would pass to the oldest daughter but she must remarry a man in her deceased husband's tribe.
- If a man dies with no sons or daughters alive, but the son's widows remain alive, then his inheritance will pass to the oldest widow by his *kinsman* that is next to him of his family, and it shall be unto the children of Israel a statute of judgment, as the LORD commanded Moses.

Numbers 27:8-11

The wife had no direct inheritance if she was childless. In that case, certain provisions (dowry) were executed to insure that she would not be destitute.

The Book of Ruth is very old, and the Tribes of Israel were living under the Law which was given at Mt. Sinai. *The sons and then daughters inherit from the deceased patriarch, but the wife does not inherit from her deceased husband.*

Almost immediately after Moses first introduced the rules of inheritance in Numbers 27, he is confronted with a problem: If females were to inherit land they might remarry outside of the tribes of Israel and the original Israelite inheritance might pass into another gentile nation. It the case of Ruth, it could even become the property of a Moabite if she remarried a Moabite. This is one reason why marriage of an Israelite woman to a non-Israelite man was discouraged. God's solution was to institute a special marriage regulation. A *widow* with no living sons who inherits from her *husband* is to be taken as a wife by her husband's nearest male kin. This guarantees that property and inheritance will automatically be retained within the family line. It is then the responsibility of the nearest male kin to both take into his house the entire family, and to sire

a male heir with the widow to inherit the land. Hence
Naomi, by Jewish law, was essentially passed by. Living in
a foreign land with foreign daughter-in-laws, she made the
only decision available to her: She would return to
Bethlehem and find the nearest male kinsman to redeem
her and her two daughter-in-laws. The rest of the story
concerns how Naomi was able to save herself and her
family.

The inheritance and control of Hebrew property is actually
more complicated than meets the eye. We will try to
describe what is happening to Naomi and her two daughter-
in-laws as simple as possible. There is an old Texas saying:
*Make things as simple as possible, but no simpler than
necessary*. The following definitions from Jewish liturgy
are needed.

- *Halakhah*….A body of laws, rituals and customs
  which define a Jew (Old Testament Scriptures, the
  Torah, the Mishnah, the Talmud)
- *Levir*…...The deceased husband's brother
- *Levirate*...The marriage of a Yevaha and a Levir
- *Yavam*….A surviving brother
- *Yabum/Yibbum*…..A Leverate marriage
- *Ketubah*…. A marriage contract

After Elimelech died, Naomi was not long in protecting
herself. Recall that she entreated her two sons to marry
Moabite women. After they did so, the family was
evidently getting along fine until tragedy struck: both of her
sons died. We have already discussed the severity of this
problem. We also need to understand the implications of
the marriage of Naomi's two sons to Ruth and Orpah. At
first glance, this might seem to be a grievous sin. Mahlon
and Chilion were both Israelites and Ruth and Orpah were
Moabites.

We fully understand a major sin that Naomi committed against Jehovah God. By agreeing (or possibly arranging) marriages between her sons and two Moabite women she surely knew that this was forbidden. However, if the Moabite women embraced the Jewish religion, they would become Jews. A conversion to Judaism is dependent on the sincerity of the convert. During their husbands' lifetimes, did Ruth and Orpah embrace Judaism? We are not told that they did so, but we will see later that when Naomi decided to return to Bethlehem, she urged both Ruth and Orpah to remain in Moab. This may have been to test their sincerity, or to save them from being rejected in Jerusalem as Moabite women. In either case, Orpah did remain in Moab, while Ruth insisted on traveling to the land of Israel with her mother-in-law to live a Jewish life. It certainly appears that Ruth was totally converted to Judaism while Orpah returned to Moab and paganism.

The Resolve of Naomi (Ruth 1:6-22)

[6] Then she arose with her daughters in law, that she might return from the country of Moab: for she had heard in the country of Moab how that the LORD had visited his people in giving them bread.
[7] Wherefore she went forth out of the place where she was, and her two daughters in law with her; and they went on the way to return unto the land of Judah.
    Ruth 9:6-7

Naomi was obviously struggling with her social and legal position in Moab. Surrounded by pagans and idol worshippers in Moab, her prospects of finding a God-fearing husband who would embrace Judaism were slim to none. In addition, there was no male left in her household.

As she languished in her fears, good news reached her ears. In Jerusalem (House of Bread) the famine had ended and once again the barley and wheat crops were growing in the fields. Naomi finally made a wise decision; she loaded up what little goods she still possessed and set out to return to her husband's land near Jerusalem with both Ruth and Orpah.

Why Naomi might have chosen to leave Jerusalem in the first place is not explained. Even though she left with Elimelech, she likely had little choice. A Jewish wife is bound to her husband and she knew the law. After arriving in Moab, over a relatively short period of time she had experienced one tragedy after another. Naomi may have chosen to repent and trust in God to honor her return, or she might have felt that to survive she had to leave Moab. This choice might have evolved as follows (*Torah sermons by Shmuel Herzfeld*).

> *Ruth is in the Land of Moab without a husband or male heir. She may have been noticed by a Moabite who possibly could have been ridiculing the Jewish woman. Imagine him saying to Naomi... "What are you doing here in Moab?" Ruth might have responded... "I came here with my husband and two sons to escape a great famine across the Jordan River in the lands near Bethlehem. My husband and two sons died, and I am left with my two daughter-in-laws. Continuing to ridicule her, the man might say: "How can you be so stupid as to still be here? Have you not heard that the famine in Israel is over and you not a Moabite?" Naomi might have reflected on this verbal assault and*

24

reached the conclusion that while the man might have just been ridiculing her, his taunting rings with truth. So, it is not hard to imagine that Naomi would seek to repent, petition God to forgive her and boldly set out to seek her kinsmen.

The Request of Naomi

[8] And Naomi said unto her two daughters in law, Go, return each to her mother's house: the LORD deal kindly with you, as ye have dealt with the dead, and with me. [9] The LORD grant you that ye may find rest, each of you in the house of her husband. Then she kissed them; and they lifted up their voice, and wept. [11] And Naomi said, Turn again, my daughters: why will ye go with me? are there yet any more sons in my womb, that they may be your husbands?
Ruth 1:8-11

We now encounter a strange directive from Naomi. She turns to her two daughters-in-law and tells them to return to Moab! Why would Naomi do such a thing? If Ruth returned to Moab, Naomi would have no further claim to her former land and holdings. She might remarry, but at her age the prospect of attracting a new, wealthy Jewish husband might be slim. It is interesting to note what Naomi said in Ruth 1:11. Naomi asserts that she is too old to bear children, but if she did by some divine act such as Sarah did with Abraham, she would need to birth a *male child*. This affirms a strange Jewish custom which was active in the time of Ruth. The family line of inheritance can be perpetuated by the mother-in-law producing *another son* to marry her daughter-in-law. This strange custom demonstrates how important it was to have Jewish land remain in the original family of inheritance. Although faced with uncertainty in Jerusalem, Naomi travelled on.

It is also not immediately clear why Ruth or Orpah would choose to leave Moab and go with Naomi back to Bethlehem. Ruth had not inherited the right to retain the estate of Elimelech, but if Naomi failed to remarry and birth a male child, she had only one hope if she left Moab: That a kinsman would reclaim the ancestral land of Elimelech and redeem Naomi, Orpah and her in Bethlehem. But things are even worse than might seem. If a kinsman decides to redeem the family of Naomi, that person also inherited any dept and legal problems associated with the estate. In addition, by Jewish laws of redemption, Ruth would need to be taken as a wife by the kinsman redeemer and then the kinsman redeemer would have to father a son with Ruth! The fate of Orpah is uncertain, but it is likely that she would also need to be taken in by the redeemer. In any case, Ruth and Orpah decided to leave Moab with Naomi.

The Choice of Ruth and Orpah

Naomi turns to Ruth and Orpah and makes a strange statement.

And Naomi said, Turn again, my daughters: why will ye go with me? Are there yet any more sons in my womb, that they may be your husband's?   Ruth 1:11

It is difficult to paint a complete picture of family law in ancient Israel. Several biblical and other sources indicate that a man's principal heirs were the *sons* born to him by his wife (or wives). However, if no sons had been produced

26

in an ancient Jewish marriage, it is the responsibility of the dead husband's brother to produce a male heir to the family land. It is pertinent to this study to realize that the dead husband's wife was not in the line of inheritance at all (Naomi). The brother of the dead husband has the obligation to marry his brother's widow (Ruth), and then produce a male heir to inherit the dead brother's property. To Western culture and even modern liberal Jewish culture, all of this seems very strange. We will explore the dilemma of Naomi and Ruth under these ancient laws later, for now note that in Leviticus 25:5 the following law was recorded.

If brethren dwell together, and one of them die, and have no child, the wife of the dead shall not marry without unto a stranger: her husband's brother shall go in unto her, and take her to him to wife, and perform the duty of an husband's brother unto her.   Deuteronomy 25:5

This is called the *Levirate Law*. A levirate marriage (*yibbum*) is mandated by Deuteronomy 25:5-6 and obliges the oldest surviving brother of a man who dies childless to marry the widow of his childless deceased brother, with the firstborn child being treated as that of the deceased brother (see also Genesis 38:8) which renders the child the heir of the deceased brother and not the genetic father.

However, if the nearest kinsman refuses to go through with the marriage, both are required to go through a ceremony known as *halizah*, involving a symbolic act of renunciation of their obligation to sustain the family line. We will discuss this later.

The Levirate Law states that if there are two brothers, and one with a wife dies, the other brother will marry the dead brother's wife. This seems strange, but actually has a deeper purpose. If she remarries into another family and has a son, the inheritance would pass to her son and leave the original family line forever. This law prevents both the extinction of the family name and loss of family land. Naomi appeals to an extension of the Levirate Law. In the story of Ruth, Naomi appeals to this law in an unusual way. In Ruth 1:11, she indicates that if she had two other sons, Ruth and Orpah would become their wife. This type of incestuous relationship was part of ancient Hebrew culture… very strange indeed. However, Naomi is not even married and has no prospects of marriage; further, she states that she is too old to marry and bear sons. Naomi now utters a strange request of her two daughter-in-laws.

Turn again, my daughters, go your way; for I am too old to have a husband. If I should say, I have hope, if I should have an husband also tonight, and should also bear sons; Would ye tarry for them till they were grown? would ye stay for them from having husbands? nay, my daughters; for it grieveth me much for your sakes that the hand of the LORD is gone out against me.   Ruth 1:12-13

Naomi is telling her two daughter-in-laws that when she returns to Bethlehem she could save the day by marrying and having a male child, which would then have to marry Ruth. Naomi says that she is too old to marry, and even if she did Ruth would have to wait years for the male child to become of age. What would happen to the estate? Why would Ruth and Oprah wait that long? How would they live and how would Jewish society treat two Moabite women? Naomi seems to be saying something very noble: *Return and save yourself, forget about me.* As good as this might sound, it is not a plausible or realistic explanation. Since Naomi was loved by both Ruth and Orpah, they could have all returned to Moab. Either Ruth or Orpah could then remarry and take care of Naomi. If Naomi is completely abandoned, she will likely live in poverty and solitude. No, there is more here than meets the eye.

Naomi would know that Elimelech had a brother in Jerusalem, and that by Jewish law he was eligible to marry Ruth as a *kinsman redeemer* (Deuteronomy 25:5-6). We will have much to say about this later, but for now we will simply say that to ask Ruth and Orpah to return to Moab would be a very poor decision for Naomi. So what prompted Naomi to insist they both return to Moab? We may never know. It might be conjectured that she was acting in the best interests of Ruth and Orpah. If Ruth went on to Jerusalem and refused to be redeemed, or if she simply could not adopt a Jewish lifestyle because of her Moabite heritage, it would create larger problems for all involved. We might give Naomi the benefit of a doubt, and assume that she was truly interested in doing what was best for two Moabite widows. Whatever the reason, we can only conjecture. For now, we note the response of Ruth and Orpah.

And they lifted up their voice, and wept again: and Orpah kissed her mother in law; but Ruth clave unto her.
And she said, Behold, thy sister in law is gone back unto her people, and unto her gods: return thou after thy sister in law.   Ruth 1:14-15

A remarkable thing happens which sets the stage for the remainder of the story. Ruth clings to Naomi and will not leave her, but Orpah decides to return to Moab and to her pagan gods. However, Ruth demonstrates a different resolve, a different spirit of belief in Jehovah God, and in her newly found Jewish faith.

And Ruth said, Entreat me not to leave thee, or to return from following after thee: for whither thou goest, I will go;

and where thou lodgest, I will lodge: thy people shall be my
people, and thy God my God:
Where thou diest, will I die, and there will I be buried: the
LORD do so to me, and more also, if ought but death part
thee and me. Ruth 1:16-17

Even after Naomi told her to leave, Ruth tells Naomi:
Where you go, I go; where you Live I will live; Your people
will be my people; and your God will be my God. These
are very strong words for a woman who was not previously
in covenant with the Almighty God. Then Ruth makes this
statement:

Where thou diest, will I die, and there will I be buried: the
LORD do so to me, and more also, if ought but death part
thee and me. Ruth 1:17

The mention of death as a separating force is the only
natural event that is capable of breaking a sincere covenant
relationship. When a man marries a woman, there is often
a vow that says something like: *till death do you part.* In
this statement, Ruth is vowing to remain committed to
Naomi until one of them dies. Because Ruth's husband had
died, she was now able to legally marry another man in
Moab. She could have chosen to go back to her family in
Moab and find another man, but she chose to trust the God
of Naomi and the fruits of her faith were tremendously
greater than she ever could have imagined.

When she (Naomi) *saw that she* (Ruth) *was steadfastly*
minded to go with her, then she left (quit) *speaking unto*
her. So they two went until they came to Bethlehem
Ruth 1:18-19a

Orpah returns to her family in Moab, but Ruth returns to Bethlehem with her mother-in-law,Naomi.

[19] *And it came to pass, when they were come to Bethlehem, that all the city was moved about them, and they said, Is this Naomi?*
[20] *And she said unto them, Call me not Naomi, call me Mara: for the Almighty hath dealt very bitterly with me.*
[21] *I went out full, and the LORD hath brought me home again empty: why then call ye me Naomi, seeing the LORD hath testified against me, and the Almighty hath afflicted me?* Ruth 1:19-21

Upon arriving, the people still remember Naomi and are excited to see her, but Naomi is depressed because she left Bethlehem with her husband and two sons and now she has returned destitute with no means of support and little hope. Naomi changes her name to *Mara* and tells people to call her that because it means, *I'm bitter*. Note that Naomi made the statement that *the Lord hast afflicted me*. It is instructive to reflect upon her attitude toward the Almighty. Naomi has no reason to blame God for all of her afflictions and hardships. She and her husband Elimelech made the choice to leave their land and home in Bethlehem, and they went to Moab of all places! Moab was a land of people who had been cursed by God for turning men of Israel to idol worship and adultery. Naomi and Elimelech did not have to go to Moab; they could have settled anywhere in other lands which God had given to Israel. Not only that, but the two sons of Naomi were allowed to marry two Moabite women. Although in reality intermarriage between Israelites and Moabites was probably quite common, several texts (Deut. 23:3, Ezra 9, and Neh. 13) either forbid or strongly discourage it. God will provide many opportunities for His people, but He will not make any decision for anyone. Free will and choice is a basic tenet of salvation and redemption. It is also what causes spiritual death and destruction if not wisely used. It is not beyond belief that the two sons of Elimelech both died prematurely because of their disobedience; we may never know.

Naomi's behavior is typical of people today who ruin their own lives and the lives of people around them. They always feel like they have been mistreated and unlucky. Any grief brought upon Naomi is her own fault. She and Elimelech left Bethlehem and all of their people of their own accord. No one told them to leave Bethlehem just because the circumstances didn't look good. She is blaming all of her misfortune on God Almighty. God surely did not tell them to leave. Their lack of faith brought them to their current state of affairs. Naomi is wallowing in a pity party, saying that her life had been one long heartache since she left Bethlehem 10 years before. She calls herself *bitter*, destitute and empty.

The Return of Ruth and Naomi

[22] So Naomi returned, and Ruth the Moabitess, her daughter in law, with her, which returned out of the country of Moab: and they came to Bethlehem in the beginning of barley harvest.   Ruth 1:22

Here we are given an interesting and important fact. Naomi and Ruth reach Bethlehem in March or April of the spring. We know this because it is in the *beginning of the barley harvest*. The people of Bethlehem who owned land were mostly an agricultural society. The grapes and figs were harvested in the month of Tishri (September/October). During this period of time the fields were ploughed and prepared for planting wheat and barley. After planting, the farmer would wait for the *early rains* which would nourish the seed and begin the growing season. The crops would then patiently remain mostly dormant until the Lord brought the *latter rains*, which would bring the precious barley and wheat crops to maturity. The barley was heartier than the wheat and would mature first. The barley crop was ready to be picked in the spring month of Nisan (March/April). This was at the time of the Jewish Feast of Passover on Nisan 14. On Nisan 15 the 7-day Feast of Unleavened Bread would begin. On the only Sunday which came around during the seven-day Feast of Unleavened Bread, the Feast of Firstfruits would begin. On that day, the High Priest would pick a *sheath of barley*, a firstfruit offering, and wave it before the Lord to be accepted as a portent of the wheat harvest to come. No wheat or barley could be picked for either sale or personal use until this occurs (Leviticus 23:9-14). The barley and then wheat would then be harvested over the next 50 days, ending on the 50th day, which is the Feast of Shavuot or Pentecost. Pentecost was also called "the Feast of Harvest" (Exodus 23:16). After Pentecost, most of the harvest was fruit: grapes, olives, dates, figs, pomegranates and numerous fruits, seeds and vegetables of lesser importance. In ancient Israel the primary harvest season extended from April through August or September. The entire harvest cycle might be subdivided into three seasons and three major crops: the *spring* grain harvest, the *summer* grape harvest and the *autumn* olive harvest. These harvests have a general correspondence with the festivals. Some grain might be harvested after Pentecost, threshing and grape-picking might overlap, and the olive harvest came both before and after the Festival of Tabernacles on Tishri 15-21 (September/October), but Tishri 1 generally marks the end of the wheat harvest season. Tishri 1 is the Jewish Feast of Trumpets. If all of this sounds familiar it should. These sequences of events are all prophetic of when Jesus Christ was crucified, buried and resurrected in 30 AD and when the harvest of all the saints will be completed on the Feast of Trumpets (Tishri 1). These prophetic truths will not be discussed here; the interested reader is referred to Phillips (**The Book of Revelation**: *Mysteries Revealed).* For now, you should only understand when Naomi and Ruth arrived in Bethlehem, *at the beginning of the barley harvest.* This must be clearly understood to properly interpret the events which follow.

The Ancestral Rights of Ruth (Ruth 2:1-23)

And Naomi had a kinsman of her husband's, a mighty man of wealth, of the family of Elimelech; and his name was Boaz. Ruth 2:1

The reader is now introduced to a man named *Boaz.* In the King James translation, Boaz is called a *kinsman of her* (deceased) *husband.* He is a member of the family of Elimelech. This observation will be extremely important as we study the ultimate redemption of Naomi and the marriage of Ruth. His social status is reflected in his title: *a man of wealth.* Ruth now begins to reveal her plan to save both her and Naomi from a life of poverty and despair.

[2] *And Ruth the Moabitess said unto Naomi, Let me now go to the field, and glean ears of corn after him in whose sight I shall find grace. And she said unto her, Go, my daughter.*
[3] *And she went, and came, and gleaned in the field after the reapers: and her hap was to light on a part of the field belonging unto Boaz, who was of the kindred of Elimelech.* Ruth 2:2-3

Recall that Naomi and Ruth returned to Jerusalem in the spring, and that the grain harvest was in full swing.

Whether it was by divine guidance or by an instruction to Ruth from Naomi, Ruth went into a field which belonged to Boaz, who was a kinsman of Elimelech. We can easily fill in some details which are not found in the narrative. Since Naomi was old and probably lacking stamina, Ruth decides to go into a field and obtain grain for their consumption. Ruth has every right to do this under the Law of God, since when fields are reaped by the landowner and his workers the field is not to be completely stripped. The reapers must leave grain around the edges of the field called *gleanings.*

When you reap the harvest of your land, do not reap to the very edges of your field or gather the gleanings of your harvest.... Leave them for the poor and the alien
Leviticus 19:9-10

It is also generally recognized that gleanings also remain in the *field* after the workers have harvested the cut wheat and barley and moved on, and if given permission by the landowner the poor and strangers can also follow after the reapers and collect grain that is left over for their family.

Gleanings are meant to feed the *poor and alien* (strangers). If this is Ruth's intent, she could pick a healthy field and simply gather up the gleanings after the workers had quit for the day. However, note carefully what Ruth now says: *glean ears of corn after him in whose sight I shall find grace.* This is a clue that Naomi actually told Ruth where to glean, in the fields of Boaz the kinsman. This conjecture becomes near certainty in Ruth 2:3. Ruth did glean in the fields of Boaz. We cannot be absolutely certain of how this came about, because we are told that *her hap was to light on a part of the field belonging unto Boaz.* One might infer that this was a fortuitous accident from this verse. However, considering all the evidence presented it is proposed that all of this "luck" was not luck at all. Here we see that Boaz is in fact part of the family of the departed Elimelech and Naomi clearly knew this from long ago.

Ruth Encounters Boaz

[4] *And behold, Boaz came from Bethlehem, and said unto the reapers, The LORD be with you. And they answered him, The LORD bless thee.*
[5] *Then said Boaz unto his servant that was set over the reapers, Whose damsel is this?*
[6] *And the servant that was set over the reapers answered and said, It is the Moabitish damsel that came back with Naomi out of the country of Moab:*
[7] *And she said, I pray you, let me glean and gather after the reapers among the sheaves: so she came, and hath continued even from the morning until now, that she tarried a little in the house.*   Ruth 2:4-7

The first thing we see is that Boaz owned a field which was outside of Bethlehem. We are not told where this land might be located, but it is clear from the narrative that it was not far away. Actually, we are told that Boaz only owned *part* of the field (Ruth 2:3) and that he was kindred to Elimelech. Ruth had as her *hap*, literally her good luck, to happen upon the portion of the field (land) that belonged to Boaz! Luck indeed; this is a confirmation that God had his hand upon Ruth and had greater things for her to do than to return to Moab with her sister-in-law,Orpah. *Hap was also likely guided by Naomi.* This is strong proof that although life might seem to be turning against you, that

God always has a purpose in mind. It is likely that God also had something in mind for Orpah also, but due to lack of commitment and faith, she turned back and forfeited her destiny. Let this be an object lesson to all Christians today. God will provide the opportunity, but the choice of seizing an opportunity is up to the individual.

When Boaz arrived to check out the harvest of his field, he addressed his workers with a common Jewish greeting: *The Lord be with you.* The workers responded according to custom: *The Lord bless thee.* Boaz immediately sees a stranger in his field which catches his eye. A woman he had not seen before was gathering gleanings from the field. Boaz inquires as to who this woman might be and discovers that she is Ruth. It is likely that Boaz had heard of Ruth because when she arrived in Bethlehem the whole town was talking about the return of Naomi with a Moabite named Ruth. While Boaz was no doubt considering this strange situation, Ruth approached him and makes an unusual request. Before we look at this request, we should describe the method by which fields were reaped of barley and then wheat.

The workers would use a *sickle* to cut down the stalks of barley and wheat: The stalks would then be bound together to form a *sheath*. The sheath would be cast to the ground and then multiple sheaths would be gathered and bundled by other workers to take to the *threshing floor* where they would be unbound and prepared for *winnowing*; which was the separation of the wheat and barley from the stalks. Anyone not a part of the landowner's family or his employees could only reap what was left lying around the field. This was to provide food for the *poor and strangers*.

Ruth 4:7 reveals an interesting turn of events which is difficult to understand. The *head servant* that was supervising the harvest identified Ruth as the Moabite who came with Naomi from Moab. This would normally result in Ruth being removed from the field, for Moabites were not to mingle with Israelites after the Balaam/Balak incident. However, the Holy Record records that not only was Ruth allowed to continue gleaning in the field of Boaz, but she was granted permission to *glean among the sheaves following after the reapers*. This was strange indeed, because those sheaves were the main harvest and not the leftover grain. Ruth is also identified as an excellent worker. She had evidently gathered from early morning to evening without rest. Even more remarkable was that after working, Ruth was allowed to *tarry a little in the house*. This was not the house of Boaz, but a small structure or tent set up near the field to permit rest and provide water to the workers after a hot, long day. Strangers were not afforded this privilege… it can be inferred that Boaz himself invited her to join them.

Boaz Protects and Comforts Ruth

[8] *Then said Boaz unto Ruth, Hearest thou not, my daughter? Go not to glean in another field, neither go from hence, but abide here fast by my maidens:*
[9] *Let thine eyes be on the field that they do reap, and go thou after them: have I not charged the young men that they shall not touch thee? And when thou art athirst, go unto the vessels, and drink of that which the young men have drawn.*
[10] *Then she fell on her face, and bowed herself to the*

38

ground, and said unto him, Why have I found grace in thine eyes, that thou shouldest take knowledge of me, seeing I am a stranger?

[11] And Boaz answered and said unto her, It hath fully been shewed me, all that thou hast done unto thy mother-in -law since the death of thine husband: and how thou hast left thy father and thy mother, and the land of thy nativity, and art come unto a people which thou knewest not heretofore.

[12] The LORD recompense thy work, and a full reward be given thee of the LORD God of Israel, under whose wings thou art come to trust.

[13] Then she said, Let me find favour in thy sight, my lord; for that thou hast comforted me, and for that thou hast spoken friendly unto thine handmaid, though I be not like unto one of thine handmaidens   Ruth 2:8-13

Ruth has been discovered by Boaz gleaning in his field (Leviticus 19:9-10), and his reaction is startling indeed. Normally the poor and strangers would only be allowed to reap from that which was not cut from the perimeter of the land and pick up anything in the field left behind by the harvesters, but Ruth had been gathering wheat and barley *in the field* following after the workers of Boaz. This is tantamount to stealing, and Ruth could be severely punished.

Ruth might attribute her good fortune to *grace*, and she could be correct. However, Boaz clearly knows that both Naomi and Ruth are kinspeople because he has no doubt heard how they chose to leave Moab. For some reason Boaz does not reveal that he knows Ruth, because Boaz states that the Lord of Israel has rewarded her by sending her to his field. Incredibly, Boaz not only overlooked her brash behavior, but actual blessed her. Boaz entreated her to continue following after his reapers, and told his workers *not to touch her* and to *share their water* with her. Ruth then said; *let me find favour in thy sight, my lord.* Since Ruth had already been showered with favors by Boaz, this is best interpreted as not a wish for favor, but as acknowledging that she had found favor and that she hoped it would continue.

Ruth now shows her humble and truthful character. She has found grace because of her cultural and religious conversion to Judaism, which having married the oldest son of Elimelech brings her to be a part of the family of Elimelech. Ruth now boldly tells Boaz that she was *not like unto one of thine handmaidens.* While not recorded in the Holy Records, Ruth must have told Boaz that she was a Moabite by birth and a Jewish convert by marriage. Maybe Ruth was asserting that she was something special! Either way, Boaz responds in a very unusual and favorable way

[**14**] *And Boaz said unto her, at mealtime come thou hither, and eat of the bread, and dip thy morsel in the vinegar. And she sat beside the reapers: and he reached her parched corn, and she did eat, and was sufficed, and left.*
[**15**] *And when she was risen up to glean, Boaz commanded his young men, saying, Let her glean even among the sheaves, and reproach her not:*
[**16**] *And let fall also some of the handfuls of purpose for her, and leave them, that she may glean them, and rebuke her not.*
[**17**] *So she gleaned in the field until even, and beat out that she had gleaned: and it was about an ephah of barley.*
Ruth 2:14-17

Boaz is obviously very impressed by Ruth; whether it is a result of her beauty, her work ethics, or her honesty. He also knows that she is a close relative through her marriage. As previously noted, in the late afternoon *at mealtime* it was the custom of a good landowner to call the reapers aside from their workday into a small tent which had been erected next to the field and join in an evening meal with wine and/or water. The meal which was served usually consisted of bread which was dipped in light vinegar, and parched corn roasted over an open fire. From previous narratives, we know that this particular meal was served by Boaz in the early stages of the barley harvest and was probably during the early days of the Feast of Weeks (Harvest). At this time, the wheat and corn was just beginning to mature, so a mixture of barley and water was poured over maturing ears of corn. This was then mixed with beans and lentils, rolled into balls, and roasted over an open fire. This mixture is called anciently *polenta* or *kali* depending upon the ratio of corn, wheat and barley.

And *she sat by the side of the reapers*. Ruth did not sit away from the reapers as a stranger, but joined them. Boaz *reached her parched corn;* better, he *served her parched corn, and she did eat, and* (she) *was sufficed* (satisfied).

Ruth by the decree and actions of Boaz had now been fully blessed to harvest in the field(s) of Boaz among his paid workers, and even asked to join them in the evening for a *family* meal. After she left, Boaz continued to show her favor. He commanded that the workers *reproach* (touch) *her not* and to *rebuke* (criticize) *her not*. Further, in a remarkable act of grace, Boaz commanded the workers to *let fall also some of the handfuls of purpose for her, and leave them, that she may glean them.* Can you imagine what the workers thought of this? Who is this woman such that we "accidentally" leave the fruits of our hard labor for a Moabite woman? Why is Ruth being treated differently? Remember that the Moabite people represented sin against

41

God, and did not deserve anything but rejection. Paul spoke of this strange turn of events in Romans 5.

*Moreover the law entered, that the offence might abound. But where sin abounded, **grace** did much more abound* Romans 5:20

This is a prophecy of things to come. Did not Jesus suffer and die on the cross for our sins? Not just for our individual sins, but for the *sins of the world* (I John 2:2). We have all sinned and are not worthy of redemption, but we are saved by *grace* and not by works lest anyone should boast. Ruth 2:14 clearly says that after her meal Ruth picked up her harvest and left to *nourish Naomi.* Here again is a remarkable prophetic picture of the New Covenant. As Christians we are saved by grace and given more than we deserve in this life; we are commanded by Christ to respond by bringing the gospel to all sinners and unbelievers, particularly to the lost house of Israel. Ruth, a *Gentile,* has been personally blessed by Boaz and she is nourishing Naomi, a *Jew*! It is not generally recognized in Christian churches today, but all Christians have a special calling to bring the nation of Israel back into a covenant relationship with God. This intimate relationship can only be achieved by the Jews believing that *Jesus Christ* is their promised *Messiah* and *redeemer,* who had long ago been prophesied to arise and take away their sins. We should never forget this high calling.

The Reaping of Ruth

Ruth 2:17 tells us that Ruth *beat out* her gleanings. Normally, the wheat and barley which had been harvested would be taken to the *threshing floor.* Threshing is the process of loosening the edible part of cereal grain from the scaly, inedible chaff that surrounds it. It is the step in grain harvesting called *winnowing*, which separates the loosened chaff from the grain.

The traditional method of winnowing grain in large quantities was to make donkeys or oxen walk in circles over the grain on a hard surface. The animals would be shod with *brass hooves*, and as the hooves passed over and through the grain the precious grain would be separated from the stalks or the chaff. Following the separation, the stalks and the grain would be thrown into the air where they separated. The threshing floor was usually put upon a hill where the cool evening breeze would separate the wheat from the chaff. The wheat was heavier and would immediately fall, while the chaff was lighter and would be carried downwind. This would form two piles; one of *chaff* and one of *wheat*. The chaff would be burned while the precious wheat would be taken into the barn.

In ancient times, small amounts of grain and wheat could be separated from chaff by hand. In the late 18th century, before threshing was mechanized, about one-quarter of agricultural labor was devoted to threshing the grain. Industrialization and automation of threshing began in 1786 with the invention of the threshing machine by a Scotsman named Andrew Meikle. Today, everything is accomplished by a machine called a *combine harvester* which harvests (cuts), threshes (gathers), and winnows (separates) the grain in one continuous process while it is still in the field.

Jesus spoke in these same agricultural terms when he spoke of His second coming in Matthew 3. The angels will harvest the field (the earth), and the wicked (chaff) will be separated from those who have accepted him for their Lord and Savior (wheat). Jesus Christ will reap the wheat (believers) from the earth in what Paul described as the *rapture* (I Corinthians 15). Jesus himself spoke of this great event to His disciples.

....Whose fan is in his hand, and he will thoroughly purge his floor, and gather his wheat into the garner; but he will burn up the chaff with unquenchable fire. Matthew 3:12

In the Book of Revelation, the Apostle John reveals the gathering of all living unbelievers in terms of reaping a field.

[14] *And I looked, and behold a white cloud, and upon the cloud one sat like unto the Son of Man, having on his head a golden crown, and in his hand a sharp sickle.*
[15] *And another angel came out of the temple, crying with a loud voice to him that sat on the cloud, Thrust in thy sickle, and reap: for the time is come for thee to reap; for the harvest of the earth is ripe.*
[16] *And he that sat on the cloud thrust in his sickle on the earth; and the earth was reaped.*   Revelation 14:14-16

This is the fulfillment of what the Apostle John spoke of in I Thessalonians 4.

[15] *For this we say unto you by the word of the Lord, that we which are alive and remain unto the coming of the Lord shall not prevent them which are asleep.*
[16] *For the Lord himself shall descend from heaven with a shout, with the voice of the archangel, and with the trump of God: and the dead in Christ shall rise first:*
[17] *Then we which are alive and remain shall be caught up together with them in the clouds, to meet the Lord in the air: and so shall we ever be with the Lord.*
                    I Thessalonians 4:15-17

Ruth 2:17 records that Ruth took the harvest that she had picked up and *beat out what she had gleaned.* In other words, Ruth winnowed the grain by hand. She recovered about *one ephod* of edible grain. An ephod is about 2/3 a bushel and would weigh about 20 pounds. Ruth had indeed been blessed in the field, but she had to exert much time and energy (about one hour) to recover the edible grain. Prophetically we should learn that winning souls to Christ is neither easy nor immediate. If we are to "reap the harvest" it will take time and dedication.

After eating, Ruth returned to the dwelling of Naomi.

Naomi Receives Ruth

[18] *And she took it* (the grain) *up, and went into the city: and her mother-in-law saw what she had gleaned: and she* (Ruth) *brought forth, and gave to her* (Naomi) *that she had reserved* (kept) *after she was sufficed* (full).
[19] *And her mother-in-law said unto her, Where hast thou gleaned today? and where wroughtest thou? blessed be he that did take knowledge of thee. And she shewed her mother in law with whom she had wrought* (worked), *and said, The man's name with whom I wrought today is Boaz.*
[20] *And Naomi said unto her daughter in law, Blessed be he of the LORD, who hath not left off his kindness to the living and to the dead. And Naomi said unto her, the man is near of kin unto us, one of our next kinsmen.* Ruth 2:18-20

It is clear that Ruth is now aware that she is part of the larger family of the deceased Elimelech and is a relative of Boaz.

[21] *And Ruth the Moabitess said, He* (Boaz) *said unto me also, Thou shalt keep fast by* (close to) *my young men* (reapers), *until they have ended all my harvest.*
[22] *And Naomi said unto Ruth her daughter in law, It is good, my daughter, that thou go out with his maidens, that*

45

they meet thee not in any other field.
[23] So she kept fast by the maidens of Boaz to glean unto
the end of barley harvest and of wheat harvest; and dwelt
with her mother in law.   Ruth 2:11-23

Ruth was faithful to her promise that she would be true to
Naomi. Ruth did not sell any of her grain, and she brought
the full measure to Naomi (Ruth 2:20). We now see that
Naomi poses an interesting question to her daughter-in-law
Ruth: *Where have you gleaned today and what have you to
show for your work?* Ruth responded that she had worked
in the field of *Boaz*. Of course, Naomi was well aware of
where Ruth had been all day. It is not clear why Naomi
continues to conceal her knowledge about what is going on.
It is obvious from the entire narrative that Naomi knew
from her previous life in Bethlehem that Boaz was a
profitable and wealthy landowner and relative, and that as
we shall see he is eligible to fulfill the role of a *Goel* or
kinsman redeemer. In my mind, it is not hard to believe that
Naomi orchestrated the whole scenario and probably told
Ruth early that morning where a *good place* to reap might
be found. In any case, Naomi will eventually decide to
reveal to Ruth that Boaz is a near kinsman. We will see
later that he cannot be the brother of Elimelech and the
nearest kinsman redeemer, but he is evidently the second in
line.

To Naomi's credit, there is no reason why we should
condemn her at all for trying to find a kinsman redeemer
for Ruth. First, Naomi is in a very tough situation. She is a
widow and probably old enough that she would not expect
a steady stream of eligible bachelors to come calling. She is
well within her moral and social rights to try and find
someone to take care of her and Ruth. Second, Ruth
(*desirable*) was by all indications a vibrant and good
looking woman who was not only pleasing to the eye, but

was not afraid to work. At this point, Naomi does what any real believer would do after hearing that her plan was working; she praised God for his goodness, kindness and mercy. In the world today, people often try to manipulate their own lives and the lives of others and take advantage of others. Usually, the sorrow and pain that comes upon us is self-inflicted. When things go bad for a believing Christian, we need to realize that we were never promised not to experience afflictions or tribulation. In all situations He is worthy of praise because He is faithful. So Naomi must be commended for praising God and giving the glory to Him.

There is a good question that we should ask ourselves every evening: *Where have I harvested today*? Have I won someone to Christ or started anyone down the path of salvation? Have I been generous with what God has given me? Have I worked *in the field* to bring forth God's kingdom, and what have been the fruits of my labors? When the Lord deals bountifully with us, let us always remember to leave *gleanings* for the poor and strangers. *The Lord loves a cheerful giver*. We must not be weary of what we are called to do, because in due season we shall rest. Ruth did not make an excuse to sit around, or to go home early; she worked until *evening* and then went home. Let us *do the works of him that sent us, while it is still day* (John 9:4).

Ruth now tells Naomi that Boaz has not only been good to her on this day, but that he gave her authority to follow after his reapers until the *entire* harvest season is over. Naomi tells Ruth that this is an unusual blessing, and that Ruth should not even consider being in another field.

Ruth continued to glean in Boaz's field for about seven weeks, until near the end of the main barley and wheat

harvests. This was around the time of *Pentecost*. Naomi
had earlier hoped that Ruth would find *rest* in the home of
another husband in Moab (Ruth 1:9), but Naomi's hope for
Ruth now centers upon Boaz, who could act as a *kinsman-
redeemer* if he can gain the privilege and chooses to do so.
In a strange turn of events, we will shortly see that Boaz is
not in a position to immediately ask Ruth to be his wife and
redeem the land of Elimelech. Boaz is not the nearest
Kinsman Redeemer. Naomi must clearly have known that
this is true, but she nevertheless concocts a plan for Ruth to
approach Boaz and not the nearest of kin. Perhaps Naomi
knows the nearest kinsman redeemer, and was certain that
he will not step up to his obligations. Perhaps God has
spoken to Naomi and given her the path to take; we will
never know.

The Preparations of Ruth (Ruth 3:1-18)

*[1] Then Naomi her mother in law said unto her, My
daughter, shall I not seek rest for thee, that it may be well
with thee?*
*[2] And now is not Boaz of our kindred, with whose
maidens thou wast? Behold, he winnoweth barley to night
in the threshing floor.*
*[3] Wash thyself therefore, and anoint thee, and put thy
raiment upon thee, and get thee down to the floor: but make
not thyself known unto the man, until he shall have done
eating and drinking.*
*[4] And it shall be, when he lieth down, that thou shalt
mark the place where he shall lie, and thou shalt go in, and
uncover his feet, and lay thee down; and he will tell thee
what thou shalt do.*
*[5] And she said unto her, All that thou sayest unto me I
will do.*   Ruth 3:1-5

Naomi realizes that Boaz is interested in Ruth. Boaz has not only noticed her, but granted her unusual and special privileges in his field. It is interesting to examine the position and age of Boaz. Ruth 2:1 has identified that Boaz was a *mighty man of wealth.* In the Hebrew Language, the term "mighty man" carries the weight of a well-respected Israelite, a leader in the community, and a man of high moral character. He is also a landowner who supports many *maidens* and *reapers.*

Although Boaz is a perfect choice to marry Ruth, he has one big thing going against him. He was probably very old when he met Ruth. We can verify from Ruth 3:10 that he was grateful that Ruth did not desire or follow after *younger men.* This does not say anything about the age of Boaz except that he was not a young man. The age of Boaz when he met Ruth has been estimated by his genealogy to be at least 90 years old and he could have been over 100 years old! We know from Ruth 1:1 that the story of Ruth took place during the time of the Judges. This was not too many years after the Exodus. During this general time period, it was not unusual for men to live more than 100 years. Aaron lived to be 123 years old (Num 33:39); Joshua died at age 110 (Judges 2:8); and Amran, who was a grandfather of Boaz, lived to be 137 years old (Ex 6:20). It is not beyond the stretch of imagination that Boaz might have even been close to 110 years old when he encountered Ruth in his field. However, he was viral enough when he married Ruth to have a son called *Obed* who was the father of Jesse who was the father of King David.

Nevertheless, Naomi continues to press the issue. Naomi asks Ruth if she should *seek rest for thee that it may be well with thee?* To *seek rest* is an idiom that implies a permanent relationship, marriage to Boaz, which would make Ruth's future secure. In fact, any marriage contract between Boaz and Ruth would also secure the future of Naomi in her old age.

Naomi now reveals a second part of her plan. First, she makes sure that Ruth understands that Boaz is a *near relative.* This will prove to be the most important thing in driving the story of Ruth to its ultimate conclusion.

Naomi tells Ruth that Boaz will be watching over his harvest on his threshing floor after the sun goes down (Ruth 3:2). Naomi tells Ruth to wash herself (*purify* her body), put on perfume (*anoint* herself), put on an attractive dress (be *desirable*) and go to Boaz after it is late. It seems that following work in the fields, Boaz was going to eat a late meal, have a few glasses of wine (Ruth 3:3) and sleep on the threshing room. (Ruth 3:7). This is not an unusual thing to do during the threshing season. Naomi had done her homework and was sure of what Boaz would be doing that evening.

Here is where it gets interesting. Boaz will sleep on the threshing floor, a common thing to do to protect his grain from robbers. After he is sound asleep, Ruth is to present herself to him. The procedure is for her to quietly uncover his feet, lie down at his feet and wait for Boaz to wake up. Ruth will then be told *what to do* by Boaz. Ruth never questions Naomi and only replies that: *All you tell me to do, I will do.*

The Methods of Ruth

[6] *And she went down unto the floor, and did according to all that her mother in law bade her.*
[7] *And when Boaz had eaten and drunk, and his heart was merry, he went to lie down at the end of the heap of corn: and she came softly, and uncovered his feet, and laid her down.*

50

[8] *And it came to pass at midnight, that the man was afraid, and turned himself: and, behold, a woman lay at his feet.* Ruth 3:6-8

The plan which Naomi has put forth to Ruth should now be examined. Is this a questionable thing to do, or is it common practice? It is difficult to believe that what Ruth has been asked to do is anything but nefarious. The fact that Ruth would sneak onto the threshing floor of Boaz while he is asleep and heavy with wine is highly questionable, but to *uncover his feet and lie there* is something that a prostitute might do. Imagine this scenario: a man today is sleeping in his bedroom and he wakes up to find an attractive woman that he recently met laying under his covers at his feet. Only two things would happen: he might jump up and run her off; or he might assume that she is seeking an intimate relationship with him. In the case of Ruth and Boaz, consider the background of Ruth. She is a Moabite; the Moabites worshipped false idols and without any guilt participated in sexual acts fueled by alcoholic beverages. This is exactly what Balak did to the men of Israel to try and destroy Israel by the wrath of God. Another extremely interesting fact when considering this portion of the story is that God's hand is clearly upon all the events recorded in the Book of Ruth. It is a Biblical fact that God can and does exercise His will in ways that cannot be understood by mortal man. This is evident in several incidents which clearly violate moral principles, but which were allowed to accomplish His master plan. A few examples will prove this point.

Abraham is the most revered patriarch in Jewish history. In a visitation from God, Abram and his wife, Sarah, are told that from his loins will arise a great nation. But Sarah and Abram were childless and as time passed both neared 100 years old. In an act of lost faith, Sarah propositioned both

51

Abram and her handmaiden Hagar to have sexual relations to produce a male heir. Both accepted, and a male child called *Ishmael* was born out of an adulterous relationship. True to God's word, even after Abram laughed at God, Ruth and Abram did conceive a male child called *Issac*. We know that nothing but trouble eventually came from the progeny of Hagar, but Jesus Christ came from the loins of Issac (Matthew 1).

Recall that as Sodom and Gomorra was being destroyed, Lot's wife looked back and was turned into a pillar of salt, leaving Lot a widower. Shortly afterward, the two daughters of Lot got him drunk and made love to him; both became pregnant and birthed a male child. The oldest daughter bore a son, and called his name *Moab*; he was the father of the *Moabites*. The younger daughter also bore a son, and called his name *Ben-ammi*; he was the father of the *Ammonites* (Genesis 19:30-38). Both became mortal enemies of Israel.

When Joshua crossed the Jordan River to conquer the Promised Land, the first obstacle encountered was the fortress city of Jericho. He sent two spies to Jericho, who upon entering the city were discovered by the soldiers. They sought refuge in a very unusual place, the house of Rahab the harlot. Not only that, Rahab saved the two spies by lying and sending the soldiers away on a wild goose chase.

There are many such stories hidden in the Holy Scriptures. Note that the Lot and Abram incidents occurred *before* the Law was given, but the story of Rahab took place *after* the Law was given. The issue is this: God is an omnipotent and a sovereign God, and His ways are so far above our understanding that we must just accept them and move on.

Although the western world today might imagine that Naomi is suggesting that Ruth take a morally questionable approach to attract Boaz, there is another possible and more likely motive for her actions that should be discussed. Some commentators have suggested that this act of Ruth was an acceptable part of ancient customs. If a woman came to a man at night, uncovered his feet, and placed her body upon the feet of the man, she was offering herself to be a bride. This custom is not recorded in the Holy Scriptures, but might well have been an acceptable practice at the time of Ruth. Note that Ruth placed herself *beneath the hem of Boaz' garment,*

In ancient times, the hem of one's garment holds great significance. Recall that when Moses set up the tabernacle at Mt. Sinai he also received instructions on how the Levitical Priesthood was to be dressed. This is fully explained by Phillips, *The Book of Exodus.* Sewn on the bottom of the hem of the white robe worn by the priesthood were four blue tassels, one attached to each corner of the robe.

The Lord said to Moses, "Speak to the Israelites and say to them: Throughout the generations to come, you are to make tassels on the corners of one's garments, with a blue cord on each tassel. You will have these tassels to look at and so will remember all the commands of the Lord, that you may obey them and not prostitute yourselves by going after the lusts of your own hearts and eyes. Then you will remember to obey all of My commands, and will be consecrated to your God. I am the Lord your God."   Numbers 15:37-41

These tassels were to remind each Jewish man of his responsibility to fulfill God's commandments and to avoid lustful thoughts of the heart. These tassels were said to be tied into 613 knots to constantly remind them of the 613 laws of Moses. The tassels were to be a constant reminder to walk according to God's Laws. The hem of a King's garment and the symbolic tassel also came to be associated with a person's authority. Recall that David humiliated Saul by sneaking up to him in a cave at the *Spring of Ein Gedi*, and cutting off Saul's tassels, which were a symbol of his kingly authority (I Sam 24:4-6). This symbolism continued even until the time of our Lord Jesus Christ. Recall that when Christ was preaching by the Sea of Galilee, great throngs of people were pressing to Him. One woman in particular with an *issue of blood* forced her way through the crowd and *touched the hem of his garment.* Christ immediately stopped and felt *virtue flow through him.* We can now know what happened on that occasion. According to Rabbinical writings, the woman was not trying to touch the robe of Jesus but the *tassels* on His robe. She had heard of the Messiah who could heal and she anxiously sought Him out. But what is the spiritual reason she wanted to touch the hem of His garment: the *tassels of His tallit* ?

These *tassels* were the very point of contact she needed to release her faith to receive a miracle in her life. What did they represent? *First,* they represented the Word of God, which is always the place where we can find healing for all of the physical ailments in our life. *Second,* the fringes also represented the *authority* of Jesus Christ. She had heard that many people had been healed by Christ; that He taught with authority; and when He spoke, people were healed. *Third,* it is also certain that she had recognized Christ as the long-awaited Messiah and that He was the Son of God. Born-again Christians today should learn a valuable object lesson from this woman. The *act* of touching the hem of Christ's garment did not heal the woman, but her *faith* did. The writer of Hebrews confirms this: *Without faith it is impossible to please God.*

It is entirely possible that Naomi knew of these things when she told Ruth to lift the robe of Boaz (lift his tassels) and lie beneath them. By doing so, she was showing her devotion to Boaz, offering herself to Boaz as his bride, and stirring upon him the notion that he could be the kinsman redeemer for both her and Naomi. The Ancient Hebrew Research Center in Jerusalem offers the following insight.

> *Boaz probably recognized the significance of this act by Ruth, but he also realized that many other Jewish men would think that this was an effort to initiate sexual contact. To protect the reputation and integrity of Ruth, he instructed her to: Let it not be known that a woman came into the floor. Boaz did not instruct Ruth to lie about their encounter; he only instructed Ruth to not speak of it. In Ruth 3:10 it is also revealed that Ruth did spend the night with Boaz, but that: She lay at his feet until morning, and she rose up before one could know the other.*
> (*Robert L. (Bob) Deffinbaugh at* **Bible.org** and the Ancient Hebrew Research Center; **http://therefinersfire.org/tallit.htm**)

No matter how the *methods* of Naomi might be interpreted, the *motive* is clear; God had a plan for Ruth and Boaz and it would come to pass. It is more than interesting that in Ruth 4:18-21 the genealogy of Jesus Christ contains Rahab, who married Salmon, who was the mother of Boaz and who was in the ancestral linage of Jesus Christ!

*My thoughts are not your thoughts, **nor are your ways My ways***, *saith the Lord.*   Isaiah 55:8

The Motives of Ruth

And he said, Who art thou? And she answered, I am Ruth thine handmaid: spread therefore thy skirt over thine handmaid; for thou art a near kinsman. Ruth 3:9

This is an important fact that Ruth now discloses to Boaz: He is a *near kinsman*. According to Ruth 2:1, Naomi knew that this was so long before Ruth gleaned in the field of Boaz, and was in fact the reason that Ruth had placed herself at the feet of Boaz. All of Bethlehem knew Ruth had returned to Bethlehem with Naomi, and Boaz had no doubt known that she was the widow of Elimelech. Naomi was a Jew by birth and from the *House of Bread*, which is Bethlehem. It is inconceivable that Boaz would not know that he was a near kin of Naomi. He would also know that Ruth was a Moabite who had committed to the Jewish faith. Although generally discouraged, it was permissible for a Jewish man to marry a Gentile.

Occasionally, a Jew marries a Gentile who then begins to believe in Jehovah God as defined and understood by Judaism. Such a convert must reject all non-Jewish theologies. Jews sometimes call such people *ethical monotheists*. Steven Greenberg, an Orthodox Rabbi, has made the controversial proposal that, in these cases, the non-Jewish partner be considered a *resident alien*; the biblical description of a resident alien is someone who is not Jewish but who lives within the Jewish community and follows all the laws and societal rules of Judaism. Such *resident aliens* share all of the same responsibilities and privileges as the Jewish community in which they reside. In fact, it is commonly believed that the blessings promised to Abraham were the sole possession of the Jews. This was not so; Gentiles could either marry into or covert to Judaism.

The Leverite Law

The problem which faced Naomi and Ruth were not primarily those of marriage, but one of inheritance. Everywhere in the ancient world, widows were a seriously disadvantaged group. Ruth had no sons and being a Moabite by birth she was particularly disadvantaged. A Jewish husband who died without a son to continue his name, land and property was considered by the Hebrews a terrible tragedy. To keep the land in Jewish possession, the law allowed a brother or another near kinsman to redeem the deceased's property by marrying his widow and *entering in to her* to produce a son to continue the family line. A monogamous marriage was preferred, but polygamy was acceptable in this particular case. Thus, if a kinsman redeemer was already married this was not a hindrance, but the kinsman would need both the resources and the desire to support a new wife.

The Laws which governed this procedure were called the *Leverite Law* and is given in Deuteronomy 25. The Leverite Law is as follows.

The Leverite Law (Deuteronomy 25:5-7)

[5] *If brethren dwell together, and one of them die, and have no child, the wife of the dead shall not marry without unto a stranger: her husband's brother shall go in unto her, and take her to him to wife, and perform the duty of an husband's brother unto her.*
[6] *And it shall be, that the firstborn which she beareth shall succeed in the name of his brother which is dead, that his name be not put out of Israel.*
[7] *And if the man like not to take his brother's wife, then let his*

Naomi was a Hebrew woman who had married another Hebrew called **Elimelech** in Jerusalem. In the midst of a great famine, Elemikech moved his wife Naomi and their two sons (**Mahlon and Chilion**) to the land of Moab. Both of the sons married a Moabite woman (**Ruth and Orpah**). Within 3 years, the father and his two sons were dead. The **Leverite Law** concerned redeeming the land and possessions which remained. If a married man died without any male children to carry on his name and inheritance, it was his brother's responsibility to marry the widow. The purpose: "The first son she bears shall carry on the name of the dead brother so that his name will not be blotted out from Israel." (Deuteronomy 25:6).

One can recognize that this ancient custom seemed to be defined by "two brothers living together". By the time of Naomi, this law evidently been expanded to include the general case of no surviving brothers. In that case, there were Rabbinic rules created which authorized *any* near male kinsman to execute the Leverite law. The nearest kinsman should perform this duty, but there was a right of refusal if desired: This was called **Hahlitzah**. If the nearest kinsman refused to carry out his duties, he was to remove his sandal in the presence of elders (reliable witnesses): The widow was then to *spit in his face* to place shame upon the nearest kinsman (Deut 25:5-10). The right of redemption was then passed on down to the next nearest kin. The relative who executed this duty was called a **Goel**. Once the widowed woman had married into the family of the Kinsman Redeemer, any son born to the redeemer and the widowed woman would become the son of inheritance of the woman's deceased husband's land and wealth.

This unusual custom actually originated with *Jehovah* God. The land did not belong to the people, it belonged to God. Israel was only the caretaker of the land. The land allocated to the 11 tribes of Israel after the Exodus was never intended to leave that tribe of Israel. The *Law of the Leverite* and the *Goel* was to make sure that the land was always possessed by a son of Israel.

Boaz was a *near relative* of Naomi's late husband, but he was not a brother. We will see that after a premeditated and planned encounter with the nearest kinsman, Boaz would perform the duties of a kinsman redeemer by marrying Ruth and buying the property that had belonged to Naomi's deceased husband, Elimelech (Ruth 4:9-10). Boaz is properly called the Kinsman *Goel*. The desired outcome of the Leverite law was to produce a son that would then be the legal heir of Elimelech's property, and this was exactly what eventually came to pass.

The earliest Biblical example of a levirate relationship is complex (*http://www.womenintheancientworld.com/ruth*) It concerned Judah's three sons: *Er*, *Onan* and *Shelah* (Genesis 38). When Er died, Judah told Onan to have children by his brother Er's widow, *Tamar*, so that Er's name would carry on. Onan, knowing that any children borne by Tamar could legally inherit all of Er's possessions, slept with Tamar but selfishly ensured that she did not have any children by *spilling his seed upon the ground*. God was so displeased He put Onan to death. Judah did not then give Tamar to Shelah as his wife; He was afraid that God might also kill Shelah.

When Tamar realized that Judah would not allow Shelah to fulfill the obligations of levirate marriage, she disguised herself as a prostitute and sat where she knew Judah would approach. Judah did not recognize her and purchased her services. Likely fueled by strong wine, Tamar became pregnant and bore Judah twin sons, Perez and Zerah.

Having been tricked into siring a son(s) to carry on the line of Er, he took the only way out available to him by declaring: *She is more righteous than I, since I wouldn't give her to my son Shelah* (Genesis 38:26). Perhaps Judah was afraid of God's wrath; perhaps he decided to repent of his actions... we will never know. Tamar could also not be commended for her actions, but she did secure a son(s) for the family legacy. In another unfathomable act of God's sovereignty and plan, through her son, Perez, Tamar became an ancestor of Jesus Christ (Matthew 1:3).

Boaz Commits to Ruth

[10] *And he said, Blessed be thou of the LORD, my daughter: for thou hast shewed more kindness in the latter end than at the beginning, inasmuch as thou followedst not young men, whether poor or rich.*
[11] *And now, my daughter, fear not; I will do to thee all that thou requirest: for all the city of my people doth know that thou art a virtuous woman.*   Ruth 3:10-11

Boaz now responds to Ruth and he does not criticize her for what she has done. Instead, it is obvious that Boaz holds Ruth dear to his heart. Boaz asks the Lord to bless her because of the kindness she has shown toward him, *more in the end than at the beginning.* Boaz has demonstrated that he is very attracted to Ruth, but when she showed up in his field he was not really sure how she might feel about him. However, the actions of Ruth toward him on the threshing floor were not viewed as immoral but one of true affection. He is obviously very concerned about their age difference, since he commends her for not seeking a much younger man. Boaz gives no clue that he thought Naomi has been orchestrating all that has taken place, and this might well be true. Boaz is convinced that Ruth is a virtuous woman because she did not press herself upon him for a sexual encounter.

And now it is true that I am thy near kinsman: howbeit there is a kinsman nearer than I. Ruth 3:12

Boaz now tells Ruth that he is indeed a *near kinsman,* but that he is not the *nearest of kin.* Boaz must now have in mind the depth and weight of the *Leverite Law.*

Tarry this night, and it shall be in the morning, that if he will perform unto thee the part of a kinsman, well; let him do the kinsman's part: but if he will not do the part of a kinsman to thee, then will I do the part of a kinsman to thee, as the LORD liveth: lie down until the morning. Ruth 3:13

Boaz entreats Ruth to stay with him for the rest of the night. While not directly stated, it is clear that Boaz will attempt to redeem Ruth the following day *if he* (the nearest kinsman) *will not perform unto thee the part of a kinsman.* This refers to whoever is the nearest of kin who has the right to redeem Ruth if he so desires. If the nearest kin is not willing to redeem Ruth, Boaz will. The plan of Naomi has worked like a charm! If Boaz will redeem Ruth, Naomi's future will also be secure.

And she lay at his feet until the morning: and she rose up before one could know another. And he said, Let it not be known that a woman came into the floor.   Ruth 3:14

We again see an undertone of the sexual implications of how Ruth approached Boaz: *She arose before one could know the other.* It is not necessarily implied that if Ruth had pressed Boaz they would have engaged in intimate activities. Rather, it is more likely that this statement reflected that both Ruth and Boaz did not wish to consummate their relationship outside of marriage. Ruth rises early the next morning to escape being detected. It is also likely that Boaz did not want her intentions to be misinterpreted, or Boaz might have been worried about his own reputation and the gossip that would fall upon him if word got out that he had slept with Ruth for the entire night.

Also he said, bring the veil that thou hast upon thee, and hold it. And when she held it, he measured six measures of barley, and laid it on her: and she went into the city.
Ruth 3:15

Boaz gives Ruth *six* measures of barley in her veil. What quantity of barley is associated with a single *measure* is not given, but it was no more than could be carried by Ruth. It is likely that there is no significance in six measures; it is probably just a simple gift to Ruth. The phrase *laid it on her* indicates that Boaz filled her veil with barley and placed it upon her head to carry it home. Women often carried heavy loads great distances in those days upon their heads. This practice is still prevalent in Africa, Egypt and other Far East countries today. Finally, the grain was identified as *barley*. This clearly verifies that these events likely took place during the Jewish Feast of Firstfruits in March or April around Nisan 15-21 before the wheat matured. Ruth returned to Naomi in Bethlehem early the next morning.

[16] *And when she came to her mother in law, she said, Who art thou* (how did it go?)*, my daughter? And she told her all that the man* (Boaz) *had done to* (for) *her.*
[17] *And she said, these six measures of barley gave he me; for he said to me, Go not empty unto thy mother in law.*
[18] *Then said she, Sit still* (do not worry)*, my daughter, until thou know how the matter will fall: for the man will not be in rest, until he have finished the thing this day.*
Ruth 3:16-17

Ruth now tells Naomi all that transpired the previous night, which included what Boaz had said: *In the morning I will see that you are redeemed* (Ruth 3:13). Remember that the Jewish day began at 6:00 PM and the morning watch at 6:00 AM.

The Redemption of Ruth (Ruth 4:1-12)

[1] *Then went Boaz up to the gate, and sat him down there: and, behold, the kinsman of whom Boaz spoke came by; unto whom he said, Ho, such a one! Turn aside, sit down here. And he turned aside, and sat down.*

[2] *And he took ten men of the elders of the city, and said, Sit ye down here. And they sat down.*   Ruth 4:1-2

That same morning, Boaz went *up to the gate*. There is no indication of what gate this might be, but it is reasonable to assume and generally understood that it was the east gate of Jerusalem. This *gate* was more than just an entrance; it was where important business took place. A large courtyard was next to the gate, and it was common that men of Jerusalem gathered there to discuss business, government and social matters. The east gate was also where legal matters were often settled, using the men who were there as legal witnesses. It is within this context that Boaz seeks to settle the issues of legally empowering the *Leverite Law*.

Boaz evidently knew that Ruth's nearest of kin would be passing through this gate in the early morning. The kinsman eventually came by the place where Boaz waited, and Boaz hailed him down. The man turned and sat next to Boaz, possibly unaware of what might be happening. Boaz then selected 10 elders from the crowd that had gathered there and bid them sit down. The 10 elders were selected to bear witness of what was about to transpire. Normally, for settlement of simple social or monetary issues only two or three witnesses would be sufficient. However, in more important matters more were used. The ten witnesses served no function but to observe whatever transaction might be taking place and verify that everything had been conducted in a fair and equitable manner. Ten witnesses were usually selected in causes of matrimony and divorce, settlement of inheritances, and to prosecute those who broke civil laws.

[**3**] *And he said unto the kinsman; Naomi, that is come again out of the country of Moab, selleth a parcel of land, which was our brother Elimelech's:*

[**4-a**] *And I thought to advertise thee, saying, Buy it before the inhabitants, and before the elders of my people.*
Ruth 4:3-4-a

Boaz here makes a strange statement. He identifies Elimelech as *our brother*. It is not clear whether this is a term identifying Elimelech as either: (1) a dear friend, (2) a brother of the kinsman, or (3) a brother to both of them. What is clear is that the kinsman is the first in line to redeem the possessions of Ruth. From the narrative, Boaz seems to be 2nd in line. The scribe further states that the land which belonged to Elimelech was not leased but *sold.* As previously discussed, the land of inheritance, whether leased or sold, would return to the original land owner on the next *Year of Jubilee*. Note that Boaz now entreats the nearest kinsman to *purchase* the land. If the nearest of kin becomes the kinsman redeemer, he inherits the right and responsibility to also redeem the land to Naomi and Ruth. This is no doubt the correct way to frame the transaction. The land could be bought by any male kinsman of Elimelech in the specific order previously discussed. If no kinsman is either willing or able to purchase the land, it could be sold to anyone. In any case, the money from the sale would be given to the widow so that she would not be destitute.

The real difficulty which presents itself in Ruth 4:3 is the statement by Boaz that Naomi is proposing to *sell the family land.* The central figure in this negotiation is *Naomi,* not *Ruth* because Naomi is the widow of Elimelech. Elimelech was the owner of the piece of land in question and thus Naomi appears to be representing the land of Elimelech. However, we need to ask a critical question. *Does Naomi really own the land since her husband and both of her sons* (who would have been the legal heirs of Elimelech's property) *died without any male siblings*? The answer appears to be *no* because there is no provision in either the Law of Moses or Torah law for a widow to inherit land from her deceased husband. Notice I didn't say that there was no *precedence* for a female to ever inherit land, because indeed the daughters of Zelophehad pled their case to Moses (because Zelophehad had no sons, only daughters) and Moses decided (as God's earthly Mediator) that in that case they *could* inherit their father's real property (Numbers 26, 27 & 36). But such is *not* the case with Naomi; the land in question did not belong to her father but to her oldest son, who subsequently died with no male heirs as previously discussed, So the land was *not* Naomi's to sell. It is likely that by saying it was Naomi's land was simply a common way of identifying the parcel of land. So, *what was Naomi's relationship to the property that is being discussed here*? After all, this is the key to understanding both Naomi's predicament and the ultimate solution revealed in Ruth 4.

First, now that we better understand the laws of land inheritance in ancient Israel, we assume that Naomi was not in legal possession of the land. For one thing, if she was in legal possession why were she and her two daughters in such distress and poverty? If she was legally in control of the land, she could have leased or sold the field herself to someone in Bethlehem and obtained income. We can, therefore assume that neither Naomi nor Ruth had sole possession of the land and that Naomi was taking the only option available to her: She and Ruth had to be saved by a *Goel* or a *kinsman redeemer* as previously discussed.

Second, it can be assumed that Naomi did not have the right to receive any income from the land (because she was not the legal heir). The land was in possession of some other unnamed person who had legally acquired it (bought it) at some earlier point in time from Elimelech when he was alive, and Naomi's arrival back at Bethlehem was to gain control of the land (either her or Ruth) through the **goel**. In other words, the actions of Naomi and Ruth concerned getting the land returned to the family or clan (redeeming it). It is now completely obvious that Naomi was well aware of the how the land could be redeemed under the Leverite Laws. We will now see exactly how Naomi and Ruth were saved from a life of grief and poverty, and how the land was redeemed back into her family.

It is instructive for us in the Western World to realize that the land given by Joshua to the tribes of Israel were to be held in perpetuity at all costs. Hence, by the time that the Book of Ruth was written, it is likely that the original rules of inheritance had been interpreted, modified and expanded to cover every case, including the complicated case of Naomi and Ruth.

Boaz now presents the right of inheritance to the nearest of kin at the City Gate in the presence of 10 witnesses. Remember that when land was either leased or sold in Israel, it was actually more like a rental agreement since all land reverted to the *original owner* or his family at the next Year of Jubilee. Even if *sold,* the *original* owner and his family still possessed title to the land.

If thou wilt redeem it, redeem it: but if thou wilt not redeem it, then tell me, that I may know: for there is none to redeem it beside thee; and I am after thee. And he said, I will redeem it. Ruth 4:4

Even if redeemed by a kinsman, the land and holdings would *not* pass to the redeemer but to the male heir (son) of the deceased original landowner. Note that in this case there are no male heirs to perpetuate land and holdings; Ruth and her (deceased) husband had no sons, and widows were never listed in the line of inheritance (see Numbers 25-27). Recall that from the Leverite Law, it is also the responsibility of the kinsman redeemer to marry the widow and produce a son.

In Ruth 4:4, Boaz informs the man that he has the rights of nearest kinsman redeemer, and Boaz now publicly states that if he does not exercise his rights *he will redeem Ruth* and the land of Elimelech. This clearly identifies Boaz as a kinsman redeemer, but not the *nearest* kinsman redeemer.

The Leverite Loophole

Then said Boaz, What day thou buyest the field of the hand of Naomi, thou must buy it also of Ruth the Moabitess, the wife of the dead, to raise up the name of the dead upon his inheritance. Ruth 4:5

Boaz then put the full weight of redemption upon the nearest kinsman. He told him that he was not only dealing with the *property* of Elimelech, he also had to *join Naomi and Ruth* to his immediate family. In addition, if someone was going to exercise the right of kinsman-redeemer towards the deceased Elimelech, he had to fulfill the duty in regard to *both* the *property* and the *posterity*. Ruth had to become the *wife* of the kinsman redeemer and he had to sire a *son* to carry on the family name of Elimelech. This is a package deal!

In Ruth 4:3-4, Boaz spoke to the first kinsman redeemer of Ruth and said: "If you want to fulfill the Leverite Law and be the kinsman redeemer, then do so. And if you accept this responsibility, tell me so and I will step aside. But if you decline, I am next in line and I will be the kinsman redeemer if you walk away from your obligation."

Initially, this man might have felt that the acquisition of additional property would be a good move. However, once he heard the entire deal, he was not willing to go through with it. Faced with having to make a decision, the near kinsman responded as follows.

And the kinsman said, **I cannot redeem it for myself,** *lest I mar mine own inheritance: redeem thou my right to thyself; for I cannot redeem it.*   Ruth 4:6

Why did the man refuse to marry Ruth? What did he mean he would *mar mine own inheritance*? A few possibilities exist. First, the man might not want to spend his own money to buy the land, marry Ruth and also care for Naomi. Second, he might have felt the increased obligation of marrying a second wife might not be accepted by his current wife. Third, perhaps the man was not as wealthy as Boaz and did not have the ability to buy the land and a spouse as well as take on the responsibility of Naomi. Fourth, he would have to purchase the land from the current land owner with his own money, and once he had fulfilled his obligation to sire a male child with Ruth, the land would then pass to that son under the original tribal name of Elimelech. Considering all the implications, this might not have been a great deal after all. How many of you would step up? In any case, the first kinsman redeemer felt that taking on another wife (which was legal in the situation of a widow in a family) and purchasing land was an obligation he could not do or was unwilling to do. Boaz immediately took the opportunity to: (1) confirm before the 10 witnesses that he was next in line, (2) exercise his right to assume the place of kinsman redeemer, (3) welcome Naomi into his current family, (4) make Ruth his wife, and (5) sire a son with his new wife, Ruth. In all of these procedures, could the nearest kinsman redeemer simply walk away with an adios? The answer is *no*.

The agreement had been reached, but the procedure now had to become legal under Jewish law. This required a testimony of truth and understanding from the 10 witnesses. Having done that, a strange ritual was then conducted.

[7] *And if the man like not to take his brother's wife, then let his brother's wife go up to the gate unto the elders, and say, My husband's brother refuseth to raise up unto his brother a name in Israel, he will not perform the duty of my husband's brother.*

[8] *Then the elders of his city shall call him, and speak unto him: and if he stand to it, and say, I like not to take her;*
[9] *Then shall his brother's wife come unto him in the presence of the elders, and loose his shoe from off his foot, and spit in his face, and shall answer and say, So shall it be done unto that man that will not build up his brother's house.*

[10] *Moreover Ruth the Moabite, the wife of Mahlon, have I purchased to be my wife, to raise up the name of the dead upon his inheritance, that the name of the dead be not cut off from among his brethren, and from the gate of his place: ye are witnesses this day.* Deuteronomy 25:7-10

This ritual in Deuteronomy 25 was directly addressing the ancient Leverite Law which assumed there were two brothers; one died and one survived. By the time of Ruth, the Leverite Law was expanded by the Rabbis, judges and priests to cover broader applications such as the redemption of a widow with no brother-in-law or sons. The sandal being removed symbolized walking through another owner's land. To make a sale of land from one person to another a legal transaction in those days, one person would take off a sandal and give it to the other (Ruth 4:7). So after the man had agreed to let Boaz buy the property, he took off one of his sandals and handed it to Boaz (Ruth 4:8). The shoe also symbolized possession, since one trods his own earth wearing shoes. On holy ground, the shoe must be pulled off. An example of this is Moses (Exodus 3:5) and today in Israel when one visits the mosques he must remove his shoes. The action of Boaz told everyone that he had bought from Naomi the property that belonged to

Elimelech and his two sons, Chilion and Mahlon (Ruth 4:9). It also signified that he had agreed to marry Ruth (Ruth 4:10).

Not only that, the widow (Ruth) was now to spit in the nearest kinsman's face! The act of spitting in ones face was to publicly rebuke and criticize the near kinsman who refused to take in his own relatives. Jewish custom is rooted upon strong loyalty to the family unit, and to refuse redemption was an insult and a social faux-pas. In latter times, the widow was to spit upon the ground rather in ones face. Isn't it interesting how *social Pressure* constantly overwhelms the commands of God?

It is more than interesting that we consider the full implication of what Jesus Christ was conveying to His disciples at the Lords Last Supper. He had His disciples remove their *shoes* (sandals) and performed the ritual of feet washing upon His disciples in spite of their objections. Traditionally, Christians have interpreted this as conveying humility and servitude as a key characteristic of a true Christian. Of course this was true, but it might have had even deeper implications in light of the Leverite Laws and Old Testament teachings. We will later return to this issue, but for now think on the truth that Jesus Christ was not the near kinsman redeemer of mankind; God the Father was the near kinsman redeemer…He created Adam and the entire human race.

Moses had to remove his shoes at the burning bush (Exodus 3:5). This was an act of honor in standing before God, but it also likely symbolized his removing any semblance of his royalty in Egypt from his life. Moses and the royal priesthood had to remove both their clothes and their shoes in the Holy Place of the tabernacle before they could serve the people of Israel. If Moses was to be the redeemer of Israel, he had to change his entire life and remain spiritually clean. This is what happens to anyone who accepts Christ as their Lord and Savior. They become a *new creature in Christ* but they must continually be *washed in the word.* Keil and Delitzsch's *Commentary on the Old Testament* summarizes the entire proceedings and will be quoted verbatim.

"The law relating to the inheritance of the land property of Israelites who died childless did not determine the time when such a possession should pass to the relatives of the deceased, whether immediately after the death of the owner, or not until after the death of the widow who was left behind.

No doubt the latter was the rule established by custom, so that the widow remained in possession of the property as long as she lived; and for that length of time she had the right to sell the property in case of need, since the sale of a field was not an actual transfer of title but simply the sale of the yearly produce until the year of jubilee.

The field of the deceased Elimelech would, strictly speaking, have belonged to his sons, and after their death to Mahlon's widow (Ruth), since Chilion's widow had remained behind in her own country Moab. But as Elimelech had not only emigrated with his wife and children and died abroad, but his sons had also been with him in the foreign land, and had married and died there, the landed property of their father had not descended to them, but had remained the property of Naomi, Elimelech's widow, in which Ruth, as the widow of Mahlon, also had a share.

Now, in case a widow sold the field of her deceased husband for the time that it was in her possession, on account of poverty, and a relation of her husband redeemed it, it was evidently his duty not only to care for the maintenance of the impoverished widow, but if she were still young, to marry her, and to let the first son born of such a marriage enter into the family of the deceased husband of his wife, so as to inherit the redeemed property, and perpetuate the name and possession of the deceased in Israel".

Upon this right, which was founded upon traditional custom, Boaz based this condition, which he set before the nearer redeemer, that if he redeemed the field of Naomi he must also take Ruth, with the obligation to marry her, and through this marriage to set up the name of the deceased upon his inheritance.

In Ruth 4: 6, the near kinsman realizes that in buying the land he would be eventually giving it to heirs of Elimelech, thereby losing not only the land but also the money used to buy the land and provide for Ruth and Naomi. This he sees as ruining his own inheritance. Perhaps he already has children from a previous marriage who, he feels, would be left insufficiently provided for in such a circumstance.

Whatever the case, he defers the right of redemption to Boaz and gives Boaz his shoe as a witness to make it official (see Deuteronomy 25:5-10). This custom itself,

74

which existed among the Indians and the ancient Germans,
arose from the fact that fixed property was taken
possession of by treading upon the soil, and hence taking
off the shoe and handing it to another was a symbol of the
transfer of a possession or right of ownership" (Keil
and Delitzsh).

Boaz took upon himself all the losses the unnamed kinsman
rejected, and the task of marrying Ruth as well as bringing
Naomi into his family. He also assumed the responsibility
of bringing forth a male child with Ruth to continue the
heritage of Elimelech. Boaz declared all of this publicly
and then married Ruth.

And all the people that were in the gate, and the elders,
said, we are witnesses. The LORD make the woman that is
come into thine house like Rachel and like Leah, which two
did build the house of Israel: and do thou worthily in
Ephratah, and be famous in Bethlehem. Ruth 4:11

The 10 witnesses pronounced a blessing upon Ruth. Boaz
evidently already had a wife, and Ruth would become his
2nd wife. When Ruth is to come to the house of Boaz, she is
to become a wife to Boaz as an *antitype* of Rachel and
Leah. Recall that Jacob took both Rachel and Leah as his
wives from Laban. Jacob then sired the 12 tribes of Israel.
Even though Rachel was the daughter that Jacob loved,
Jacob also took Leah as his wife.

Boaz is told to be *worthy* of God's blessings as he dwelt in *Ephratah*, which is an ancient name for Bethlehem found in Micah 5:2.

[12] *And let thy house be like the house of Pharez, whom Tamar bare unto Judah, of the seed which the LORD shall give thee of this young woman.*   Ruth 4:12

According to the Book of Genesis, *Pharez* was the son of Tamar and Judah, and the twin brother of Zerah (Matthew 1:2). Pharez in Hebrew means *breach or burst forth*. Our Lord Jesus Christ arose from the loins of Pharaz. The Book of Ruth lists Perez as being part of the ancestral genealogy of King David (Ruth 4:18-22).

(27) *And it came to pass in the time of her travail, that, behold, twins [were] in her womb.*

(28) *And it came to pass, when she travailed, that [the one] put out [his] hand: and the midwife took and bound upon his hand a scarlet thread, saying, This came out first.*

(29) *And it came to pass, as he drew back his hand, that, behold, his brother came out: and she said, How hast thou broken forth? [this] breach [be] upon thee: therefore his name was called Pharez.*

(30) *And afterward came out his brother, that had the scarlet thread upon his hand: and his name was called Zarah.*   Genesis 38:27-30

The Lineage and Legacy of Ruth (Ruth 4:13-22)

[13] *So Boaz took Ruth, and she was his wife: and when he went in unto her, the LORD gave her conception, and she*

bare a son.

[14] *And the women said unto Naomi, Blessed be the LORD, which hath not left thee this day without a kinsman, that his name may be famous in Israel.*

[15] *And He shall be unto thee a restorer of thy life, and a nourisher of thine old age: for thy daughter in law, which loveth thee, which is better to thee than seven sons, hath born him.*

[16] *And Naomi took the child, and laid it in her bosom, and became nurse unto it.*

[17] *And the women her neighbors gave it a name, saying, There is a son born to Naomi; and they called his name Obed: he is the father of Jesse, the father of David.*

Ruth 4:13-17 reveals several things of interest. *First,* in Ruth 4:13, we learn that Boaz and Ruth did birth a son even though Boaz was well-advanced in age. This was no doubt predetermined by God. Ruth had been married to Mahlon for ten long years in Moab without conceiving a child. As in many of the matriarchal and patriarchal stories in Genesis (Genesis 16; 20-21; 25:19-26; 29:31-30:24), the Lord decides when and to whom a child will be born. *Second,* several women of Bethlehem who are with Ruth in childbirth bless the Lord God of Israel for this birth. *Third,* they recognize and understand that this child will be the legitimate kinsman who will inherit the land of Elimelech, not Boaz. *Fourth,* a prophecy is given to Naomi that: (1) the son will *restore* life to Naomi, make her feel wanted, (2) He will nourish Naomi as they grow old, provide an abundance of barley and wheat from the ancestral fields of Elimelech, and (3) he will be known (famous) throughout all Israel. Oh, that every male child would be blessed with such a prophecy!

Ruth has accepted Boaz as her husband and submitted herself to him in hopes of birthing a son of promise. This did, in fact, come to pass, and one might expect that Ruth would assume the position of the family mother. Naomi would simply be swept up in all of these wonderful events and live a life in the shadows of Ruth and her new son. However, God is gracious and blesses *His children* in ways that we cannot even comprehend. We are told that the newborn child is laid upon the bosom of Naomi and even in her advanced age Naomi was able to help raise the child! The women then declared to Naomi that the *child* would be more of a blessing to Naomi than if she had birthed seven sons. Ruth's love and loyalty to Naomi is in reality what makes this new child so dear to Naomi.

Ruth 4:17 ends the story of how Naomi and Ruth were redeemed by Boaz. The women who were the neighbors of Boaz got together and named the boy-child, *Obed*. Obed means *serving* or *one who serves*. The child was likely named eight days after his birth when he would have been circumcised. It was common for friends and family to gather on this occasion and celebrate. It was not unusual for the honored guest to suggest a name for the child. Ruth 4:17 states that *they, the women who were her neighbors, gave it a name.* Of course, this is impossible since only the maternal parents could name the child. The women only suggested a name which was then given to the child by Ruth and Boaz. The Jewish historian Josephus properly recorded the event. He said that: *The name of Obed was given to Naomi by the advice of her neighbors, who then recommended it to the parents* (Antiq. L: 5:9:4). This custom continued until the time of Jesus Christ (Luke 1:59).

This Holy Record concludes with a strange statement: *There is a son born to Naomi.* This is obviously an idiom which simply states that a son has been born to be nurtured and kept as if it was the natural son of Naomi. We are now told that Obed grew to manhood, married and had a son called *Jessie,* who begat King David, who was in the direct linage of our Lord Jesus Christ.

We cannot fail to recall another remarkable fact that David's great-grandmother was a *Moabite.* We might wonder how only a few generations later, the descendant of a Moabite woman becomes the King of Israel when Deuteronomy 23:3 strictly prohibited the descendants of Moabites from entering the congregation of the Lord for ten generations. The Jewish Rabbis explained this clear violation of God's Law as follows. *"The Jewish Midrash implies that this prohibition related only to the women who wed Moabite males, not to Moabite women who married a Jewish male and converted to Judaism"* (*Bible Reader's Companion,* note on Ruth 1:4). The Book of Ruth ends with the following genealogy.

[18] *Now these are the generations of Pharez: Pharez begat Hezron,*
[19] *And Hezron begat Ram, and Ram begat Amminadab,*
[20] *And Amminadab begat Nahshon, and Nahshon begat Salmon,*
[21] *And Salmon begat Boaz, and Boaz begat Obed,*
[22] *And Obed begat Jesse, and Jesse begat David.*
      Ruth 4:18-22

We are tempted to just accept this genealogical record as simply historical or as a postscript to a fine story. However, Ruth 4:18-22 is far more important than most commentators recognize. Why does the genealogy start with Perez?

It is because Perez was the founder of the branch of Judah's family that took his name, to which Elimelech and Boaz belonged (Numbers 26:20). Jesus Christ was said to be born in the Tribe of Judah. He is the Lion of Judah prophesied from ancient times.

This genealogy emphasizes how God circumvented custom and tradition in providing Israel's greatest ruler, King David. Like Perez, Boaz was the descendant of an Israelite father named *Salmon*, and a Canaanite harlot named *Rahab* (Matthew 1:5). Both Ruth and Rahab entered Israel because they believed and valued God's promises. It is also interesting that David was the youngest rather than the eldest son of Jesse. It is more than interesting that a harlot and a Moabite were in the lineage of Jesus Christ. The message to be learned is that Jesus Christ can take even the most sinful person and use them for His Kingdom. This is in no place more evident than in the conversion and sanctification of Saul of Tarsus, who became the greatest missionary for Christ that ever lived.

The wording and content of the genealogy does not necessarily imply that this is a complete list (consider I Chronicles 2:5-15; Matthew 1:3-6; and Luke 3:31-33).

We might also have expected Mahlon, rather than Boaz, to be mentioned since, by marrying Ruth, Boaz perpetuated the line of Mahlon, Ruth's former husband. Evidently the genealogy goes through Boaz because Boaz was the biological father of Obed.

We will now fully explore the prophetic structure of the Book of Ruth, and how the entire story provides a deeper understanding of how the Church of Jesus Christ (Gentiles and Jews) is called to redeem all of Israel.

Part 2: Prophecy in the Book of Ruth

The prophetic nature of the Book of Ruth can only be completely understood by looking backward through time to the time at which it was written. In order to fully understand the types and shadows in the book of Ruth, one must understand the antitypes. Christians today have the advantage of looking back across the Cross of Calvary and the sacrificial death of Jesus Christ, all the way to when God called Abram (Abraham) out of Ur of the Chaldee and the Nation of Israel was called forth to be God's chosen people. In Jeremiah 11 we are told that the Nation of Israel is typed as a *Green Olive Tree*

The Olive Tree of Jeremiah

*The LORD called thy name, a **green olive tree**, fair, and of goodly fruit: with the noise of a great tumult he hath kindled fire upon it, and the **branches of it are broken**. For the LORD of hosts, that planted thee, hath pronounced evil against thee, for the evil of the house of Israel and of the house of Judah, which they have done against themselves to provoke me to anger in offering incense unto Baal.*
Jeremiah 11:16-17

The context of this passage is part of a lamentation by Jeremiah that the Nation of Israel had fallen into apostasy and Baal worship:

And changed the glory of the uncorruptible God into an image made like to corruptible man, and to birds, and four footed beasts, and creeping things Romans 1:23

God made a covenant with the people of Israel at Mt. Sinai that: (you) *shall ye be my people, and I will be your God*: He would lead them out of Egypt, vanquish their foes, and give them the Promised Land. However, this covenant promise was *conditional*. The children of Israel must: *Obey my voice, and do them, according to all which I command you: so shall ye be my people, and I will be your God.* Jeremiah prophesied for more than 40 years, and he warned the people of Israel of impending doom if they did not repent. The children of Israel were typed as branches on a *green olive tree*, full of good fruit (deeds) and beautiful in God's eyes. Eventually, because of disbelief, sin and rejection of God's plan for Israel the branches (apostate Israel) were *broken off;* individual Children of Israel (branches in the good olive tree) were broken off from the promises and protection of Jehovah God.....

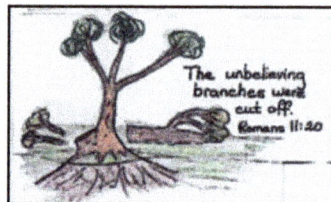

Israel a green olive tree - fair and of good fruit. Jer. 11:16

The unbelieving branches were cut off. Romans 11:20

The culmination of Israel's apostasy was the division of the United Kingdom upon King Solomon's death into the Northern Kingdom of Israel and the Southern Kingdom of

Judah. Within 500 years, Israel had fallen to the Assyrian Empire and Judah had fallen to the Babylonian Empire (the *Diaspora*). Because of disbelief God had removed His mantle of protection. But god was not through with Israel.

The Diaspora took place about 1000 years after the Law was given at Mt Sinai, but about 2500 years earlier, God had made an *unconditional covenant* with

There shall come forth a Shoot out of It's roots.
Is. 11:1

Abraham. He had promised that He would send a Messiah to Israel which would heal their wounds and deliver salvation to the Jews.

The Story of Ruth took place during the time of the Judges, about 100 years after the Exodus from Egypt took place. The Book of Ruth was probably *written* sometime during the reign of King David, and many Biblical scholars propose that the Book of Ruth was penned by Samuel. When King David died, the United Kingdom passed to the rule of his son, King Solomon. Upon the death of King Solomon, the Kingdom was ripped into two pieces: The Northern Kingdom called *Israel,* and the Southern Kingdom called *Judah.* The *branches broken off* of this olive tree represented the defeat and dispersion of both the Northern Kingdom of Israel by the *Assyrian Empire,* and the defeat and deportation of the Southern Kingdom of Judah by Nebuchadnezzar and the *Babylonian Empire.*

Although the branches were broken off, the *trunk and root* of the tree still remained and were still holy.

God had exercised divine judgment upon the Nation of Israel, but He had not abandoned the children of Israel. Israel was still the chosen people of God, and He would yet redeem them and bring them into a covenant relationship with Him. Corporately, the branches were broken off but some would be grafted back into the tree by believing in faith that a messiah would arise to redeem them.

The Dry Bones of Ezekiel

The prophet Ezekiel was a contemporary of Jeremiah who arose in the latter years of Jeremiah. When the Kingdom of Judah fell to the Babylonian Empire, Jeremiah fled to Egypt where he died. Ezekiel was deported to Babylon where he continually reminded Israel of her sins, but he also prophesied of the restoration of Israel to the land promised to Abraham and his descendents. This will finally come to pass sometime in the future during the 1,000-year Millennial Kingdom. Perhaps the best known prophesy of Ezekiel depicted the nation of Israel as a nation of *dry bones*. These bones would *live again* (resurrection). The *branches* which were broken off in Jeremiah's prophecy were the same as the dry bones of Ezekiel, but they were in two different groups. Some branches that were broken off would remain broken off and die (disbelieving Jews); other branches broken off would be grafted back into the good Olive Tree and live again. How were these branches (individual Jews) restored (grafted back) to the good tree? Those who will be saved would be saved just as Abraham was saved…. By faith in believing that a Messiah (Jesus Christ) would arise and redeem (restore) them to Jehovah. God had not rejected all of Israel, but He would yet redeem his chosen people… all who would believe His promises to Abraham… all who died in faith that God would save them from sin. After the Messiah (Christ) arrived and paid the price to nullify sin on the Cross of Calvary, the (corporate) Jews rejected Him as the promised Messiah. They could not see and would not see…. Paul said they were *blinded in part.* Some did believe both *before* the 1st coming of Christ, and *after* the 1st coming of Christ. We call these believers Messianic Jews. Those Jews who died in faith believed that a Messiah would arise to redeem them from the grave are the dry bones that will again live. They are the faithful seed of Abraham…. *Abraham believed by faith and it was accounted to him as righteousness* (Romans 4:9).

[1] The hand of the LORD was upon me, and carried me out in the spirit of the LORD, and set me down in the midst of the valley which was full of bones,
[2] And caused me to pass by them round about: and, behold, there were very many in the open valley; and, lo, they were very dry.
[3] And he said unto me, Son of man, can these bones live? And I answered, O Lord GOD, thou knowest.
[4] Again he said unto me, Prophesy upon these bones, and say unto them, O ye dry bones, hear the word of the LORD.
[5] Thus saith the Lord GOD unto these bones; Behold, I will cause breath to enter into you, and ye shall live:
Ezekiel 37:1-5

*For the LORD will not **cast off** his people, neither will he forsake his inheritance.*   Psalms 94:14

*[26] And so all **Israel** shall be saved: as it is written, There shall come out of Sion the Deliverer, and shall turn away ungodliness from Jacob.*   Romans 11:26

The Wild Olive Tree of Jeremiah was a prophetic picture of how the Nation of Israel was called to be God's chosen people. The branches were destined to bear much fruit. But the corporate Nation of Israel rejected God, apostatized, fell into idol worship and was *temporarily* cast off by God. In the Book of Romans, the following parable was presented by the Apostle Paul to confirm and expand upon this scriptural truth.

The Parable of the Two Trees

[1] I say then, Hath God cast away his people? God forbid. For I also am an Israelite, of the seed of Abraham, of the tribe of Benjamin.
[2] God hath not cast away his people which he foreknew. Wot ye not what the scripture saith of Elias? How he maketh intercession to God against Israel, saying,
[3] Lord, they have killed thy prophets, and digged down thine altars; and I am left alone, and they seek my life.
[4] But what saith the answer of God unto him? I have reserved to myself seven thousand men, who have not bowed the knee to the image of Baal.
*[5] Even so then at this present time also there is a **remnant according to the election of grace**.*
[6] And if by grace, then is it no more of works: otherwise grace is no more grace. But if it be of works, then is it no

86

more grace: otherwise work is no more work.

[7] *What then?* **Israel hath not obtained that which he seeketh for; but the election hath obtained it, and the rest were blinded**

[8] *(According as it is written, God hath given them the spirit of slumber, eyes that they should not see, and ears that they should not hear;) unto this day.*

[9] *And David saith, Let their table be made a snare, and a trap, and a stumbling block, and a recompense unto them:*

[10] *Let their eyes be darkened, that they may not see, and bow down their back.*

[11] *I say then,* **Have they stumbled that they should fall? God forbid: but rather through their fall, salvation is come unto the Gentiles,** *for to provoke them* (Israel) *to jealousy.*

[12] *Now if the fall of them be the riches of the world, and the diminishing of them the riches of the Gentiles; how much more their fullness?*

[13] *For I speak to you Gentiles, inasmuch as I am the apostle of the Gentiles, I magnify mine office:*

[14] *If by any means I may provoke to emulation them which are my flesh, and might save some of them.*

[15] **For if the casting away of them be the reconciling of the world, what shall the receiving of them be, but life from the dead?**

[16] **For if the firstfruit be holy, the lump is also holy: and if the root be holy, so are the branches.**

[17] *And if some of the branches be broken off, and thou* (gentiles), *being a* **wild olive tree**, *were grafted in among them, and with them partake of the root and fatness of the olive tree;*

[18] *Boast not against the branches. But if thou boast, thou bearest not the root, but the root thee.*

[19] *Thou wilt say then, The branches were broken off, that I might be grafted in.*

[20] *Well;* **because of unbelief they were broken off,** *and thou standest by faith. Be not highminded, but fear:*

[21] *For if God spared not the natural branches, take heed lest he also spare not thee.*

[22] *Behold therefore the goodness and severity of God: on them which fell, severity; but toward thee, goodness, if thou continue in his goodness: otherwise thou also shalt be cut off.*

[23] ***And they also, if they abide not still in unbelief, shall be grafted in: for God is able to graft them in again.***

[24] *For if thou wert cut out of the olive tree which is* **wild** *by nature, and were grafted contrary to nature into a* **good olive tree***: how much more shall these, which be the natural branches, be grafted into their own olive tree?*

[25] *For I would not, brethren, that ye should be ignorant of this* **mystery***, lest ye should be wise in your own conceits; that* **blindness in part is happened to Israel, until the fullness of the Gentiles be come in***.*

[26] *And so all Israel shall be saved: as it is written,* **There shall come out of Sion the Deliverer***, and shall turn away ungodliness from Jacob:*   Romans 11:1-26

The *good olive tree* is the Olive tree of Jeremiah, which in its original state represented both faithful and unfaithful *Jews*. The *wild olive tree* represents the *gentiles*, who by the grace of God and through the new covenant… by faith… will be grafted into the good tree. It will now be stated that the story of

Braches(Gentiles of faith) Grafted into the Good Olive Tree

The Wild Olive Tree

The Good Olive Tree

Ruth foreshadowed and prophesied of Romans 11:1-26 Paul called this a **mystery** not revealed until that time. That is why the prophetic structure of Ruth can only be understood looking back from when Paul penned the Book of Romans.

There are two trees revealed by Paul: one is the Green Olive Tree described in Jeremiah 11 called the **good olive tree** (Romans 11:24), and the other is called the **wild olive tree** (Romans 11:17). The good olive tree is Israel including the *elect of Israel* who by faith believed that their salvation was by a coming Messiah, and those Jews who had followed strictly after the works of the law but eventually accepted Christ as their redeemer. They are the branches that have been *grafted back into the good tree*.

The *wild olive tree branches* that are grafted into the original good tree represent the *Gentiles* who by faith have believed that Jesus Christ is the long-awaited Son of God who takes away the sins of the world and offers eternal life.

And if ye (Gentiles) *be Christ's, then are ye Abraham's seed, and **heirs** according to the promise.*   Galatians 3:29

Salvation and redemption is offered by faith to Jews and Gentiles alike, for *without faith it is impossible to please God* (Hebrews 11:6). The chosen ones, the elect, have always been saved by *faith* from Adam to until some future point in time when the *fullness of the gentiles have come in.* The good olive tree is identical to the olive tree in Jeremiah 11.

Once again, it is important to fully understand what God has been doing for almost 6000 years. God planted the Good Olive Tree (Israel). The root of the good olive *tree is holy*, and if the root is holy so are the *branches that will grow upon the tree* (Romans 11:16). Paul reveals that *some* (not all) of the branches were broken off (Romans 11:17). Why would holy branches be broken off? ..... because of *unbelief* (Romans 11:20). The original branches of the tree represented corporately and individually the nation of Israel. After the Exodus from Egypt and the land was conquered, Israel became mired in unbelief; turning to adultery and falling into idol worship and apostasy. The United Kingdom which started under King David became corrupt to the point that David was not allowed to build the temple of God. Solomon was granted this privilege but he also became unfaithful. The mighty United Kingdom was divided into two kingdoms. Both would be destroyed in less than 500 years. The branches were broken off of the holy tree; however, God was not through with Israel, the roots were still there, and there was always a remnant that died in faith of a coming Messiah to redeem them from the law.

Through the years, other branches grew and other branches were broken off until Jesus Christ came to the River Jordan to start His Messianic Ministry. John the Baptist declared:

*And now also the axe is laid unto the **root** of the trees*
Matthew 3:10

Was the Nation of Israel abandoned by God? God forbid.

I say then, Have they (Jews) *stumbled that they should fall?
God forbid: but rather through their fall* (Jews) *salvation is
come unto the Gentiles, for to provoke them* (Jews) *to
jealousy.*   Romans 11:11

The Apostle Paul goes on to explain a great **mystery**.
Through disbelief, rejection and *stumbling* the Jews (Holy
branches) were cut off the *natural olive tree* and the *wild
olive branches* (Gentiles) were grafted into the holy tree.
Why? ..... to provoke them to jealousy. But *if the root is
holy, then the branches are holy* (Romans 11:16). Under
the New Covenant there are no Jews or Gentiles, but only
the *ecclesia* or a believing remnant. The scriptures teach us
that the *good* olive tree was not taken up, destroyed and
replaced by the *wild* olive tree but its roots remained
planted and secure. The roots (Abraham, Isaac and Jacob)
by God's grace still give nourishment to those *old branches*
(believing Israel) which remain and the *new branches*
(gentiles) which have been grafted into the good tree. The
new branches represent both gentile and Jewish believers
who have accepted Jesus Christ as their Lord and savior.
There are those who teach what is called *Replacement
Theology*. This teaches that the church has displaced and
replaced Israel. This is not what is taught by the Apostle
Paul.

[18] *Boast not against the branches. But if thou boast, thou
bearest not the root, but the root thee.*

91

[19] Thou wilt say then, The branches were broken off, that I might be grafted in.

[20] Well; because of unbelief they were broken off, and thou standest by faith. Be not highminded, but fear:

[21] For if God spared not the natural branches, take heed lest he also spare not thee.

[22] Behold therefore the goodness and severity of God: on them which fell, severity; but toward thee, goodness, if thou continue in his goodness: otherwise thou also shalt be cut off.

[23] And they also, if they abide not still in unbelief, shall be grafted in: for God is able to graft them in again.
Romans 11:18-23

The roots of the good tree nourish and support both the old branches (faithful Jews) which remain and the new branches (gentile believers) which have been grafted into the tree, for Christ was a Jew by birth of the Tribe of Judah and was of the *seed of Abraham.*

*[9] What then? are we better than they? No, in no wise: for we have before proved both **Jews** and Gentiles, that they are all under sin;*

*[29] Is he the God of the **Jews** only? Is he not also of the Gentiles? Yes, of the **Gentiles** also:*   Romans 3:9, 29

Those Jews of Israel who by lack of *faith* rejected Jesus Christ as their long awaited Messiah were the branches that were cut off: For *without faith it is impossible to believe God* (Hebrews 11:6). Those Gentiles who accept Jesus Christ as their Savior are the branches which have been grafted into the good tree. Those branches which were cut off were the result of *unbelief* in Jesus Christ who would arise as the long awaited Jewish Messiah and would take away the sins of the entire world. It must be understood that the branches and roots in Jeremiah 11 are the same tree that God planted, and it still grows today; it is eternal and holy. Many of the original branches are still there; they are the Old Testament patriarchs who died in faith. New branches (Jews and gentiles) have been grafted into the good tree.

Genesis 15:6 tells us that Abraham, *believed in the LORD; and He reckoned it to him as righteousness.* This reckoning by faith was fourteen years before God commanded Abraham to be circumcised, and 430 years before God gave the law to Moses. Therefore, he was neither justified by works or by obeying the Law. He was redeemed and justified in the same way that every person is redeemed and justified...... by *faith.*

It is instructive and interesting to understand the practice of grafting limbs into a tree. The natural branch will be cut off at an angle, and the unnatural limb to be grafted into the branch will be cut in the same manner, both parallel to the rings (veins) of the two pieces. They will then be bound together exactly matching the veins in both the limb and the branch. Hence, the tree into which a branch has been grafted cannot tell the difference in the old and new limb. The roots of the tree supply nourishment and life to the new branches just as it did for the original branches. In addition, the practice is always to cut off the original (bad) branches of the tree and graft in the new (good) branches. Paul was using this fact correctly when he stated:

*For if thou wert cut out of the olive tree which is wild by nature, and were grafted contrary to nature into a **good olive tree**: how much more shall these, which be the natural branches, be grafted into their own olive tree?*
Romans 11:24

The grafting of Gentiles into the tree of the Jews was *contrary to nature*. By this we see that the Jews (good branches) should have entered into an eternal covenant relationship with God, but they rebelled and rejected both Him and His Son Jesus Christ. The wild branches (Gentile believers) had to be grafted into a covenant relationship with God through a contrary method. God had to send His only begotten son to save a sinful world. The Gentiles were redeemed from sin through Jesus Christ, but they cannot boast or claim that Israel has been rejected.

[23] *And they also, if they abide not still in unbelief, shall be grafted in: for God is able to graft them in again.*
[24] *For if thou wert cut out of* **the olive tree which is wild** *by nature, and were grafted contrary to nature into a* **good olive tree***: how much more shall these, which be the natural branches, be grafted into their own olive tree?*
Romans 11:23-24

Paul assures us that God is not through with Israel.

[25] *For I would not, brethren, that ye should be ignorant of this mystery, lest ye should be wise in your own conceits; that blindness in part is happened to Israel, until the fullness of the Gentiles be come in.*
[26] *And so all Israel shall be saved: as it is written, There shall come out of Sion the Deliverer, and shall turn away ungodliness from Jacob:*   Romans 11:25-26

The unbelieving branches were cut off. Romans 11:20

There shall come forth a shoot out of it's roots. Is 11:1

There are three important things which Romans 11:25-26 teaches us:

1. This was a *mystery* until the Apostle Paul revealed it in his letter to the Romans.

   Recall that Paul had written the Book of Romans to believers in Rome who were backsliding into Judaism. Paul was trying to assure them that Christ had not replaced God, but that He was the Son of God sent to redeem all mankind…Jews and Gentiles alike… by taking away the sins of all believers; past, present and future. When Christ settled the sin issue, the way to redemption and salvation was clearly only by faith in Jesus Christ. He was able to save anyone who would believe upon His name; that he was the Son of God; and that if He was resurrected from the dead those who believe in Him will be resurrected also. How simple can it be!

2. Israel has been blinded *in part* until the *fullness of the Gentiles come in.*

   Israel has not been cast off or permanently rejected: *God forbid.* Corporate Israel has just been *temporarily cut off* from the good tree and *blinded in part* until the fullness of the Gentiles are brought into the body of Christ; until every Gentile that has and will accept Jesus Christ as their savior has been grafted into the holy tree. But not just Gentiles will be redeemed:

   *For by one Spirit are we all baptized into one body, whether we be **Jews** or Gentiles, whether we be bond*

or free; and have been all made to drink into one
Spirit. I Corinthians 12:13

3. God has not cast away His chosen people (Israel).
    He will graft the Jewish branches by *faith* back into
    the good tree

Not all individuals were blinded (rejected and crucified
Jesus Christ), but the rejection was by *corporate Israel*.
There has always been a *remnant* of believers. Today, we
see more and more Jewish believers accepting Jesus Christ
as their savior. This is what Paul meant when he revealed
that: *And they also, if they abide not still in unbelief, shall*
be grafted in: for God is able to graft them in again
(Romans 11:23). This grafting back into the good tree is
happening today, but it will reach its ultimate fulfillment in
the last days of the *Tribulation Period*. During this period
of time, many Gentiles will be martyred and many Jews
will be won to Christ by the church saints. When the
Rapture of the Church removes all Christians and leaves all
Jewish unbelievers behind, Israel will finally see that Jesus
Christ was their long-awaited Messiah and will turn to Him
for their redemption.

*And so **all Israel** shall be saved: as it is written, There shall*
come out of Sion the Deliverer, and shall turn away
ungodliness from Jacob. Romans 11:26

*And I will gather the **remnant** of my flock out of all*
countries whither I have driven them, and will bring them
again to their folds; and they shall be fruitful and increase.
Jeremiah 23:3

*Yet will I leave a **remnant**, that ye may have some that*
shall escape the sword among the nations, when ye shall be
scattered through the countries. Ezekiel 6:8

*And it shall come to pass, that whosoever shall call on the name of the LORD shall be delivered: for in mount Zion and in Jerusalem shall be deliverance, as the LORD hath said, and in the **remnant** whom the LORD shall call.*
   Joel 2:32

The Jewish remnant who survives the terrible Wrath of God (the 7 Bowl Judgments) will finally inherit the land which God promised Abraham and Moses, and they will dwell in the land for 1000 years.

*But they shall sit every man under his vine and under his **fig** tree; and none shall make them afraid: for the mouth of the LORD of hosts hath spoken it.*   Micah 4:4

For I do not desire, brethren, that you should be ignorant of this mystery, lest you should be wise in your own opinion, that blindness in part has happened to Israel until the fullness of the Gentiles has come in. And so all Israel will be saved, as it is written: "The Deliverer will come out of Zion, and He will turn away ungodliness from Jacob".
Romans 11:25-26

In the eternal plan of God, there are currently in this Age of Grace only two types of people in the world: believers in the Lord Jesus Christ and unbelievers. These born-again believers (Jews and Gentiles) are called the *ecclesia* or the body of Christ.

In Romans 11:25-26, Paul once again reassures us that God is not through with Israel. The completion of God's purposes with the Gentiles marks His renewed grace to the people of Israel. After the time of the Gentiles has been fulfilled, (the great Tribulation period of time), then *ALL ISRAEL* will be saved and the *times of refreshing* (restoration) *shall come from the presence of the Lord.* (Acts 3:19, Romans 11:25-26).

The phrase *all Israel will be saved* has generated much confusion. This cannot possibly mean *all* of Israel since the time of Abraham will be saved. The Apostle Paul suddenly shifts from Christ's 1st coming to a Messianic prediction of His 2nd advent. After the great tribulation period described in the Book of Revelation, Christ will return from His heavenly home to save Jerusalem from Satan and his followers at the Battle of Armageddon. At this point in time, those Jewish believers who are still alive will all realize that Christ is their long awaited Messiah, and *all of Israel will be saved......* all who remain. This will be the last group of people on earth who will have the opportunity to accept Jesus Christ as their Lord and Savior. J. C. Ryle in 1867 made the following observations:

The Jews are kept separate that they may finally be saved, converted and restored to their own land. They are reserved and preserved, in order that God may show in them as on a platform, to angels and men, how greatly he hates sin, and yet how greatly he can forgive, and how greatly he can convert. Never will that be realized as it will in that day when "all Israel shall be saved".

The Book of Ruth is not only venerated among the Jews, but it is also an important part of the Christian King James Biblical record. The Book of Ruth is part of the Jewish *Hamesh Megillot.* Even today, it is read on the Feast of Shavuot which celebrates the main harvest. It is sad that most Christians fail to appreciate or understand the role that the Torah and the Old Testament plays in understanding the New Testament. A Christian believes that anyone who accepts Jesus Christ as their Lord and Savior will receive the gift of eternal life and the forgiveness of sin by grace. Most Christians think that the Old Testament is not relevant to Christianity except to provide historical context. This is unfortunate, since the God who chose Israel as his chosen people is the same God that sent His only Son to save a sinful world. The Old Testament provides tremendous truths concerning what God likes and dislikes, and the punishment of ignoring His laws. The *Torah* or the Pentateuch (Genesis, Exodus, Leviticus, Numbers and Deuteronomy) means *instruction, guide or teaching.* The book of Genesis sets a foundation for the entire Bible, and should be carefully studied by every Christian. The Torah and the Law no longer holds us in bondage, but that does not imply the law was not holy and good. Jesus Christ told us that:

[17] *Think not that I am come to destroy the **law**, or the prophets: I am not come to destroy, but to fulfill the law.* [18] *For verily I say unto you;* ***Till heaven and earth pass away***, *not one jot or one tittle shall in no wise pass from the **law**, till all be fulfilled.* Matthew 5:17-18

*Knowing that a man is not justified by the works of the **law**, but by faith in Jesus Christ, even we have believed in Jesus Christ, that we might be justified by the faith of Christ, and not by the works of the **law**: for by the works of the **law** shall no flesh be justified.* Galatians 2:16

The sacrificial death of Christ on the cross of Calvary did not abolish or disallow the law, but it enabled every Christian to live under the curse of the law without condemnation. This being true, should not all Christians carefully study and understand the Torah and the Old

Testament? The answer, of course, is *yes*. The Old Testament was not only written for the Jews, but to foreshadow in types the coming Messiah and redeemer Jesus Christ. Almost everything in the Old Testament was not just Jewish, but also spoke of Jesus Christ. So, we would certainly expect Christ to be prophesied in the Book of Ruth. If the Book of Ruth is about the redemption of Israel and salvation by faith and grace, and not just a love story between Ruth and Naomi, then we should carefully consider the prophetic message in this short but great book.

Prophetic Shadows and Types

The Book of Ruth is certainly a love story between Naomi and Ruth, but it is much more. Ruth loved Naomi so much that she was willing to leave her family and her friends to go with Naomi back to Jerusalem. The words of Ruth when she committed to this decision are ones of beauty and dedication. They have been repeated down through the years at countless marriage ceremonies.

And Ruth said, Entreat me not to leave thee, or to return from following after thee: for whither thou go, I will go; and where thou lodge, I will lodge: thy people shall be my people, and thy God my God: Where thou die, will I die, and there will I be buried: the LORD do so to me, and more also, if ought but death part thee and me. Ruth 1:16-17

Many authors and biblical scholars have recognized that the Book of Ruth was prophetic in nature. There have been sermons preached and books written which interpret and explain the Book of Ruth beyond its obvious context. It should be restated that the events recorded in the Book of Ruth actually happened long ago and covered a period of time just over 10 years in duration. If the Book of Ruth is prophetic, what are the types and antitypes which can be found in the story?

> In this context a *type* is defined as: A person, thing, action, event, ceremony, structure, furniture, number, etc. in the Old Testament that prefigures a corresponding antitype in the New Testament. A type is also sometimes referred to as a *shadow* or *reflection* of the reality it represents. **The initial occurrence is called a shadow or type and the fulfillment is designated the antitype.**

With this definition of types and antitypes let us present the prophetic message hidden in the Book of Ruth. There have been many books written about the story of Ruth, but the majority have recognized only a simple prophetic structure. *Boaz* has been pictured as a type of our Savior and redeemer, Jesus Christ. *Naomi* is a type of Jewish Israel, and *Ruth* is a type of the Church. This seems a plausible assumption at first glance. Boaz and Christ were both Jews by birth. Both were from the tribe of Judah. Christ was the redeemer of both Jews and Gentiles; Boaz was also a redeemer. Ruth was a gentile, and Naomi was a Jew. While the identification of Boaz as a type of Christ is certainly believable, is it the best interpretation of the Book of Ruth? In subsequent analysis, there may be an even better way to type Boaz. We should dig deeper to discover the true prophetic message in the story of Ruth. We will now show that the entire Book of Ruth and all of its main characters are prophetic, but not as obvious as it might seem.

The Book of Ruth has historically been identified as a true story. On the surface, it seems to document how Elimelech, a Jewish land owner who lived in or near Bethlehem, deserted his inheritance by leaving his land and moving to the Land of Moab with his wife Naomi and their two sons. Elimelech and his two sons die, leaving Naomi and her two daughters-in-law (Ruth and Orpah) in Moab. Naomi leaves Moab with Ruth and Orpah, but Orpah turns back. The remainder of the story tells of how Naomi and Ruth are saved from a life of poverty and grief by a near kinsman called Boaz. However, it is also a touching love story between Ruth and Naomi. Before we begin to identify types, let us conduct a short review of the facts.

A time of great famine afflicted the land around Bethlehem. In an act of desperation, fueled by a lack of faith, Elimelech took his wife Naomi, their two sons (Mahlon and Chilion), and journeyed to the Land of Moab. There Mahlon and Chilion married two Moabite women called Ruth and Orpah. During a subsequent period of 10 years, Elimelech, Mahlon and Chilion all died, leaving Naomi, Ruth and Orpah all widows. Naomi decided to return to Bethlehem, and took Ruth and Orpah with her. On the way to Bethlehem, Naomi entreated both Ruth and Orpah to return to Moab. In one of the great displays of love ever recorded, Ruth refused to go and pledged herself to Naomi. Orpah turned away, and was never mentioned again.

The rest of the story centers on how Naomi sought for her and Ruth to be redeemed and accepted back into the Jewish society and religious structure of Israel. We are introduced to a man called Boaz who invoked an ancient ritualistic right called the *Leverite Law* to become the *Goel* or the kinsman redeemer. Boaz would eventually save Naomi and Ruth from a life of despair and poverty, and redeem the ancestral land of Elimelech. Boaz takes Ruth as his wife, and they sire a son named Obed. The story concludes with a genealogy that shows Obed became the grandfather of King David. Eventually, our Lord Jesus Christ would come from his lineage.

The story of how Boaz redeemed Naomi and Ruth is the finest and most complete example of the Hebrew custom of kinsman redemption in all of the Holy Scriptures. From this beautiful story we will now see that three important things emerge: (1) The relationship between Ruth and Boaz provides New Testament believers a deeper understanding of how Christ relates to the Church and its individual members, the Body of Christ, His bride; (2) The Book of Ruth provides a typology of how Israel relates to the Church and the role that the Church will play in restoring Israel into a covenant relationship with God, and (3) How all of Israel will eventually be redeemed by Jesus Christ the Son of God.

The Book of Ruth goes far beyond the relationship between Israel and Jehovah God; it shows how the Son of God working through the Gentiles will one day redeem Israel. As is often the case, the Holy Spirit will use the Book of Ruth to convey eternal truths as well as historical events. The Apostle Paul tells us in his letters that the Old Testament was enacted and written not only to record a history of the Hebrews, but to reveal to Israel a coming Messiah who would redeem not only them but also take away the sins of the entire world. ***The Jews have been and always will be God's chosen people.*** Because of God's mercy, we Gentiles and the Church have been grafted into the *Good Olive Tree* by the grace of our Lord Jesus

Christ. Israel was the natural branches which were broken off because of apostasy and disbelief, but they will be grafted back into the tree when they finally realize that Jesus Christ is their long-awaited Messiah. Meanwhile, New Covenant believers have been grafted into the tree, nourished by the holy roots. In Amos 9:12, the descendants of David (the Jews) and the Gentiles are categorically differentiated and named as joint occupiers of the millennial kingdom on earth where Christ will reign in Jerusalem. In the Dispensation of Grace which we now live in today, God only recognizes two different types of people: (1) Those who do not believe in Jesus Christ as the Son of God, and (2) The *ecclesia* or those who believe that Jesus Christ is their Lord and Savior and the Son of God. Salvation is offered by grace to both Jews and Gentiles. In the fullness of time, a Jewish believing remnant will turn to Christ as their long-awaited Jewish Messiah.

[9] *I will sift the house of Israel among all nations, like as corn is sifted in a sieve, yet shall not the least grain fall upon the earth.*
[10] *All the sinners of my people shall die by the sword, which say, the evil shall not overtake nor prevent us.*
[11] *In that day will I raise up the tabernacle of David that is fallen, and close up the breaches thereof; and I will raise up his ruins, and I will build it as in the days of old:*
[12] *That they may possess the remnant of Edom, and of all the heathen, which are called by my name, saith the LORD that doeth this.*
[13] *Behold, the days come, saith the LORD, that the plowman shall overtake the reaper, and the treader of grapes him that soweth seed; and the mountains shall drop sweet wine, and all the hills shall melt.*

[14] *And I will bring again the captivity of my people of Israel, and they shall build the waste cities, and inhabit them; and they shall plant vineyards, and drink the wine thereof; they shall also make gardens, and eat the fruit of them.*
[15] *And I will plant them upon their land, and they shall no more be pulled up out of their land which I have given them, saith the LORD thy God.*   Joel 4:9-15

[16] *Let no man therefore judge you in meat, or in drink, or in respect of an holyday, or of the new moon, or of the sabbath days:*
[17] *Which are a shadow of things to come; but the body is of Christ.*   Colossians 2:17-18

Following His Resurrection, the Savior taught His disciples to look to the contents of the Scriptures; in other words the *Old Testament*, and see all things concerning Him.

And beginning at Moses and all the prophets, he expounded unto them in all the Scriptures the things concerning himself.   Luke 24:27

Part III: Ruth through a New Prism of Prophecy

We will now reexamine the Book of Ruth through the prism of prophecy. After Joshua crossed the Jordan River, he entered into a 7-year campaign of acquisition and conquest. Joshua then divided the land among the 11 tribes of Israel (The tribe of Levi received no land).

The story of Ruth begins in Bethlehem (*House of Bread*), which is about 3-4 miles southwest of Jerusalem (*House of Peace*). The *ancestors* of both Mary and Joseph were from Bethlehem, which was in the territory assigned to the tribe of Judah (Matthew 2:6).

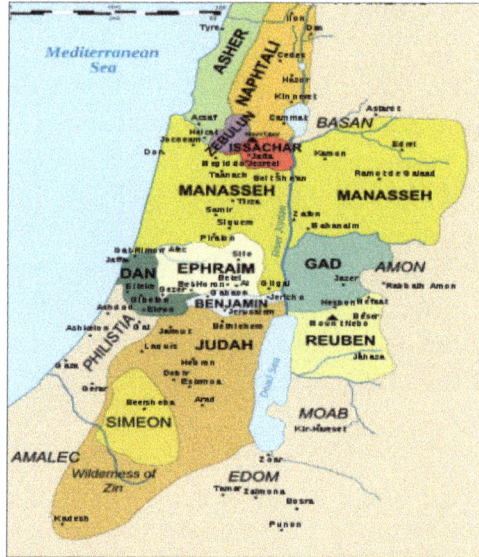

The Book of Ruth is traditionally read in the Jewish Synagogues on the 2nd day of Shavuot. There are many explanations given for the reading of Ruth on this day. The most-quoted reason is that Ruth's coming to Israel took place around the time of Shavuot, and her acceptance into the Jewish faith represented acceptance by the Jewish people of the Torah. The Jewish religion does not recognize the prophetic significance of the Book of Ruth because they fail to recognize that Jesus Christ is their long-awaited Messiah. The Apostle Paul explained why corporately the Jews have rejected Christ.

*For I would not, brethren, that ye should be ignorant of this **mystery**, lest ye should be wise in your own conceits; that blindness in part is happened to Israel, until the fullness of the Gentiles be come in.* Romans 11:25

In the Scriptures, a *mystery* is something that was completely unknown until it was written down by an apostle or a prophet. A mystery is always something previously hidden, but now revealed in due time. The mystery revealed by the Apostle Paul in Romans 11:25 is that Israel has been *blinded* but only *in part* until the *fullness of the Gentiles* has come in. Paul reveals another mystery in his letter to the church at Colossi.

*[26] Even the **mystery** which hath been hid from ages and from generations, but now is made manifest to his saints: [27] To whom God would make known what is the riches of the glory of this **mystery** among the Gentiles; which is Christ in you, the hope of glory:* Colossians 1: 26-27

The *Mystery* hidden from the Jews is that through Christ Jesus a New Covenant came in which the **Ecclesia or the body of Christ** is to be composed of *both* Jews and Gentiles. Almost all of the gentiles who compose the body of Christ today will fail to see that Christ Jesus came to fulfill the Abrahamic Covenant and that as part of that fulfillment the gentiles will be heirs and joint-heirs to all of God's promises. This will continue until the *fullness of the gentiles* comes to pass. It is blindness in part that has prevented the Jews (and most gentile saints) from understanding the full prophetic message contained in the Book of Ruth.

The Book of Ruth is much more than a historical love story between Ruth and Naomi, it is also about how Naomi returned to Israel to redeem her family land. It is also a prophetic but hidden story of how the Jews and Gentiles would become heirs to the promises made to Abraham. The Book of Ruth is about the redemption of a believing Jewish remnant which will be saved by grace, and of how the Gentiles have become heirs and joint heirs through the sacrificial death and resurrection of the promised Messiah, Jesus Christ The prophetic truths found in the Book of Ruth are not easily found, but can be recognized with careful study and the help of the Apostle Paul and his letters to the Romans, Colossians and Ephesians.

A Brief Review

To preface what we are about to reveal, recall that *Elimelech*, his wife *Naomi*, and his two sons *Mahlon* and *Chilion* were living near Bethlehem on the ancestral land of Elimelech. There came a famine upon the land, and Elimelech and all of his family left Israel and settled in the Land of Moab. Both Mahlon and Chilion took Moabite wives named *Ruth* and *Orpah*. Within 10 years Elimelech, Mahlon and Chilion all died, leaving Naomi, Ruth and Orpah widowed and destitute. Not only were Naomi, Ruth and Orpah left without any visible means of support, there were no male children to inherit the ancestral land of Elimelech and the family holdings. Realizing their desperate situation, Naomi, Ruth and Orpah leave Moab and set out to Bethlehem. On the way, Orpah turns back to Moab, and Naomi and Ruth continued on to Bethlehem. Both arrive in the spring during the wheat harvest season. Upon arriving in Bethlehem, Naomi prompts Ruth to glean in the fields of Boaz, who is a near kinsman to Naomi. Ruth finds favor with Boaz, and is allowed to glean wheat with the reapers, even sharing in their meals. Naomi next sends Ruth to the threshing floor of Boaz, where she places herself beneath the feet of Boaz, a ritual in which Ruth offers herself to Boaz in marriage. Boaz accepts Ruth's offer but realizes that simple marriage to Ruth will not redeem her, Naomi, and the ancestral land of Elimelech. To redeem the land and possessions of Elimelech, Boaz must marry Ruth under an ancient rite of marriage called the *Leverite Law* in which the nearest kinsman is expected to marry the widow. However, Boaz is only a *near* kinsman and not the *nearest* kinsman. Boaz approaches the nearest kinsman in another ancient rite, and the nearest kinsman declines to marry Ruth. This allows Boaz to legally reclaim the ancestral land of Elimelech by marrying Ruth. But there is another problem. Boaz cannot simply marry Ruth and have her inherit the ancestral land of Elimelech. Land is passed down under the Leverite Law to a *male*. Hence, Boaz must marry Ruth and *sire a son* to redeem the land. Even though he is well advanced in age, Boaz does just that producing a son named *Obed*. Obed inherits the land and rescues Naomi in the process. In a strange turn of events which shows the sovereignty of God, the Book of Ruth ends with a genealogy of Obed which will later show that Jesus Christ is of the lineage of not only King David but also of Obed!

Using this short summary as an introduction, we will now show how the *Book of Ruth* prophesies of not only the redemption of Jewish Israel believers who died in faith of the coming Messiah Jesus Christ, but of the faithfulness of God who will restore Israel to the promised land; and of how Jews and Gentiles alike will be heirs of all the promises to Abraham and his faithful seed.

The Town of Bethlehem *(House of Bread)*

In Ruth 1:1 we are told that Elimelech and his family dwelt in or very near the town of Bethlehem *(house of bread)*. Bethlehem was where our Lord and Savior Jesus Christ was born by divine appointment. Bethlehem was only about 3-4 miles south of Jerusalem, where King David was to reign over Israel. The City of Bethlehem represented **corporate Israel**, and its inhabitants were composed of *both* apostate Jews and the faithful seed (plural) of Abraham, who died in faith looking forward to a Messianic redeemer. The believing remnant will be heirs to the Abrahamic Covenant and all of the promises. Old Testament saints were clearly saved in the same way the New Testament saints are saved, by *faith* alone, by the *Grace* of God, and by and through the *redemptive work* of Christ.

For what does the Scripture say? "And Abraham believed God, and it was reckoned to him as righteousness." Now to the one who works, his wage is not reckoned as a favor, but as what is due. But to the one who does not work, but believes in Him who justifies the ungodly, his faith is reckoned as righteousness, just as David also speaks of the blessing upon the man to whom God reckons righteousness apart from works: "Blessed are those whose lawless deeds have been forgiven, and whose sins have been covered.

"Blessed is the man whose sin the Lord will not take into account."   Romans 4:3-8

Elimelech (My God is King)

The LORD called thy name (Israel) *a **green olive tree**, fair, and of goodly fruit*   Jeremiah 11:16-a

This olive tree represents the *Nation of Israel*. In the example of the trees in Romans 11, the Apostle Paul called this a *Good or Natural olive tree*. The main roots represent Abraham, Isaac and Jacob (Exodus 3:15). The branches represent the *Children of Israel*, God's chosen people. The branches were to be rich with beautiful leaves and much fruit. The tree was planted by God, and so the *roots* were holy. If the root is holy, so are the *branches*.

The Apostle Paul in the *Parable of the Two Trees* teaches that if the people of Israel (the Holy branches) are disobedient and unfaithful, they will be broken off. *Elimelech* is an example of these fallen branches. *First,* Elimelech chose to leave his land near Bethlehem; he did not put his trust in God to deliver him from the famine. *Second,* he chose to live in the Land of Moab, which had been cursed by God. *Third,* he allowed his sons to marry Moabite women, which was strictly forbidden.

An Ammonite or Moabite shall not enter into the congregation of the LORD; even to their tenth generation shall they not enter into the congregation of the LORD for ever   Deuteronomy 23:3

Elimelech was a perfect type of *disobedient and unbelieving Israel*. The actions of Elimelech can only be understood as an act of disobedience and *lack of faith*. Throughout the Old Testament, the Holy Branches (obedient Israel) remained on the tree, but the unholy natural branches were *broken off.*

It is interesting that the name Elimelech meant *my God is King*, which revealed the paradox of his actions. He wanted to take matters into his own hands and not put his trust in God. Elimelech was not only a type of disobedient and unfaithful Jews, but of how the entire nation of Israel fell into disobedience as well. Shortly after the story of Ruth took place, the nation of Israel rebelled against God's sovereignty by declaring:

*In those days there **was no king** in Israel, but every man did that which was right in his own eyes.* Judges 17:6

[19] *Nevertheless the people refused to obey the voice of Samuel; and they said, Nay; but we will have a **king** over us;*
[20] *That we also may be like all the nations; and that our **king** may judge us, and go out before us, and fight our battles.* I Samuel 8:19-20

Prophetically, Elimelech was a type of disobedient and unfaithful Israel, but recall that he had two sons, Chilion and Mahlon, who followed his disobedience. *Chilion* was a *type* of the *Northern Kingdom* and *Mahlon* was a *type* of the *Southern Kingdom* which separated the disobedient and United Kingdom of Solomon into two separate kingdoms: the Northern Kingdom of Israel, and the Southern Kingdom of Judah. Both eventually fell into Idolatry, apostasy and disbelief; their branches were broken off.

Man was created to exercise free will; and Naomi, Chilion and Mahlon exercised that free will by leaving with Elimelech. Their *branches* were **all** *broken off* and they lived for 10 years in disbelief and disobedience. We will see later that Naomi represented *repentant Israel*. She was grafted back into the Holy Tree of Israel; and Ruth represented the *Gentiles* who were a wild olive branch grafted into the tree of Israel. Elimelech left Bethlehem and took his family with him to Moab, which had been cursed by God.

*An Ammonite or **Moabite** shall not enter into the congregation of the LORD; even to their tenth generation shall they not enter into the congregation of the LORD for ever:*   Deuteronomy 23:3

Elimelech chose to leave the land that was given to him by Joshua, and not put his trust in God. We do not know how many other Jews left Israel to seek refuge in a foreign land, but we can safely assume that Elimelech was not the only one who left the Land of Promise. He not only left Israel (Bethlehem), but he chose to go to Moab of all places! Elimelech not only left the Land of Promise, but he risked losing his inheritance if he died without any living male heirs, which he did. It is clear from the biblical record that Elimelech was deliberately and absolutely disobedient to God's commands. It is even more clearly evident that Elimelech had lost his faith in God's promises. The Apostle Paul addressed all of the unfaithful Jews when he wrote to the church at Corinth.

There hath no temptation taken you but such as is common to man: but God is faithful, who will not suffer you to be tempted above that ye are able; but will with the temptation also make a way to escape, that ye may be able to bear it.
I Corinthians 10:13

113

It can now be easily seen that Elimelech was a type of disobedient *and unbelieving Israel*. Elimelech was not only a type of disobedient and unbelieving Jews, but his actions are exactly opposite to his calling. The name Elimelech means *my God is King*. Elimelech died in Moab; *He was a type of the branches on the good tree that were broken off and not grafted back into the good tree.*

Mahlon (diseased or sick) **and Chilion** (perishing)

The two sons of Elimelech were well beyond the first age of reason. We do not know how old they were when they left Israel, but they were old enough and mature enough to seek out and marry Moabite women. It is not clear how much wisdom Mahlon and Chilion were taught by their father, but it might be inferred that they were not grounded in strong faith. Numbers 14:18 tells us that the iniquities of the father are often passed down to the *third and fourth generations*. Regardless of any ancestral curse, man was created with full moral choice and each will be judged on his/her own faith. Mahlon and Chilion were just as bad as Elimelech; they chose to go to Moab of their own free will; they could have stayed in Bethlehem and tended the land; they even took Moabite women as their wives. Just like Elimelech, Mahlon and Chilion were seeds of disobedience. It can easily be determined that like their father Elimelech, Mahlon and Chilion were also *types of disobedient and unbelieving Israel*. They were also a type of the branches on the good tree that were broken off and not grafted back into the good tree.

As is the fate of all unbelievers, Mahlon and Chilion died twice. One was a spiritual death and the other was physical death; both were dead within 10 years.

To distinguish the two sons from the father, it can also be recognized that Elimelech, Mahlon and Chilion were also a type of King Solomon and his two rebellious and apostate sons. King Solomon, once so full of wisdom and faith, sinned and died in rebellion against God's laws. Upon his death, the United Kingdom of Israel split into two pieces; the Northern Kingdom under his son Jeroboam, and the Southern Kingdom of Judah under his son Rehoboam. Within 500 years both kingdoms had perished and had been scattered to the four winds (the *Diaspora*).

Naomi *(The pleasant or lovely one)*

Naomi left Bethlehem with her husband Elimelech and her two sons. They were all guilty of not trusting God for their deliverance. They all lacked the faith of Abraham, for *without faith it is impossible to please God* (Hebrews 11:6). The family of Elimelech was a type of unbelieving Israel; they were the *branches of the good tree that were broken off*. Elimelech and his two sons all died in Moab. The two sons had actually married Moabite women. The three of them all died in a foreign land: They were the branches of the good tree that were broken off; they withered and died in disbelief and lack of faith; they were not grafted back into the Good Olive Tree. However, there is something different about Naomi. She was also among the branches of the good tree of Israel which were *broken off*, but she decided to return to her God and his chosen people. Because she turned back to God and asked for forgiveness, she is a type of those branches of the good olive tree that were broken off but by the grace of God will be *grafted back into the tree*. Naomi was a type of the *unbelieving remnant of Israel that was grafted back into the good tree after being broken off*. It is obvious that she never completely lost all of her faith in Jehovah. Naomi admitted that she was representative of those *branches* which were broken off, but by faith those branches would be *grafted back into the good olive tree*. It seems in Ruth 1:20-21 that Naomi recognized that God had afflicted her because of disobedience. She left as Naomi (Pleasant) and she returned as Mara (Bitter). Why was Naomi so bitter? Although her two sons had died, she had received grace from God by not perishing in Moab. She did not perish in disbelief, and she was moved to repent and go back home to Bethlehem. The Hebrew root for Mara is *Marar*. It can mean bitter but can also mean severely grieved. In an interesting play on words, it might imply that Ruth was bitter at losing her husband and two sons, but she was grieved in the spirit because of her previous lack of faith. It is also interesting that when she returned, the family of Elimelech, all of her friends had recovered from the 7-year famine and were doing quite well. They received her with joy just as any repentant sinner is received by true believers. In type, we not only recognize Naomi as the Jewish believer who had fallen away from faith and subsequently repented, but she also represents the one sheep that was lost on the hills far away (Moab), but was found and restored to the arms of the good Sheppard (Matthew 18:12-14).

Naomi was *Jewish* and Ruth was a *gentile*. In the Book of Romans, Paul made it clear that salvation had come to the Gentiles through the covenant that God had made with the Jewish patriarch, Abraham. God made an unconditional promise to *Abraham* that his *seed* would redeem the sins of the whole world.

*Now to Abraham and his seed were the promises made. He saith not, and to seeds, as of many; but as of one, And to thy **seed**, which is **Christ**.* Galatians 3:16

[28] *There is neither Jew nor Greek, there is neither bond nor free, there is neither male nor female: for ye are all one in Christ Jesus.*
[29] *And if ye be Christ's, then are ye Abraham's seed, and heirs according to the promise.* Galatians 3:28-29

The return of Naomi (Jew) with Ruth (Gentile) is a beautiful example of how salvation and forgiveness of sins has come to the Gentiles through Jesus Christ (a Jew).

That the blessing of **Abraham** *might come on the* **Gentiles** *through Jesus Christ; that we might receive the promise of the Spirit through* **faith**.   Galatians 3:14

It should now be perfectly clear that Naomi is a type of the branches of the good tree that were *broken off, but that by faith were grafted back into the good tree.*

A question that also needs to be asked is: *When did Naomi turn back to God and His promises?* It is clear that Naomi repented when things in her life were about as bad as they could get. This is a prophetic type of how all Israel will suffer in the Great Tribulation to come, but they will eventually accept Jesus Christ as their long-awaited Messiah and be saved by grace. In the tribulation period, documented by the Apostle John, the Children of Israel will be persecuted more severely than any other time in history, including by Hitler and the 3rd Reich. When Christ raptures out the church (believing Jews and Gentiles) and returns in all of his glory, the Jews will finally recognize that Jesus Christ is the seed (singular) of Abraham which will redeem all of Israel who by faith believed upon His name. It is no mere coincidence that Naomi returned to Bethlehem in the spring at the time of the wheat harvest. A common theme surrounding the 2nd coming of Christ is that the wheat harvest is the gathering of all believers in the end times (Revelation 14:15-16), Hoshea 6:11, Parable of Wheat and Tares, Matthew 13:24-30).

The Reapers

From the previous discussion, the Christian today who has accepted Jesus Christ as their savior should realize that every effort should be made to bring all unbelievers to salvation by grace and faith in Jesus Christ: Not only Gentiles, but all those of Jewish faith who are lost in unbelief. Christ said over 2000 years ago: *The fields are ripe unto harvest* (John 4:35). We should now understand the full meaning of the great commission.

Go ye unto all the world, and preach the gospel to every creature.   Mark 16:15

*[37] Then saith he unto his disciples; the **harvest** truly is plenteous, but the laborers are few;*
*[38] Pray ye therefore the Lord of the **harvest**, that he will send forth laborers into his **harvest**.*   Matthew 9:37-38

The Ecclesia or the body of Christ is the laborers, and we should commit all of our time and resources to bringing both Jews and Gentiles to salvation in Jesus Christ.

*And let us not be **weary** in well doing: for in due season we shall reap, if we faint not.*   Galatians 6:9

Ruth came to the fields of Boaz where she reaped with the laborers who Boaz had placed in the field. Recall that Ruth did not gather wheat from the gleanings left along the fence rows, but she reaped *beside and among* the reapers. The reapers are a type of those who have been saved by faith and grace, and who willingly and faithfully carry out the commands of Christ to seek out and save the lost: Jews and Gentiles alike.

Ruth *(Friend)* and Orpah *(Turning Back)*

Naomi leaves the Land of Moab with Ruth and Orpah, but along the way a strange thing happens. Naomi tells both Ruth and Orpah to turn back to Moab. Orpah does return to Moab to die in sin as an unbeliever, but Ruth continues on to Bethlehem (House of Bread) with Naomi. In the synoptic gospels, Christ is revealed as the *bread of life*. Ruth is to partake of this holy bread as a *Gentile*. It should be very clear that *Orpah* is a type of millions of *Gentiles* who refuse to believe that Jesus Christ is the Son of God and that he died for our sins as the perfect sacrificial lamb on the cross of Calvary. By turning back, Orpah is rejecting

118

Christ and all of the Abrahamic promises. Ruth clearly decides to believe God's word and return to Bethlehem with Naomi. The resolve of Ruth is not just a product of her love for Naomi. She is truly converted back into the Jewish beliefs.

[16] And Ruth said, Intreat me not to leave thee, or to return from following after thee: for whither thou goest, I will go; and where thou lodgest, I will lodge: thy people shall be my people, and thy God my God:
[17] *Where thou diest, will I die, and there will I be buried: the* **LORD** *do so to me, and more also, if ought but death part thee and me.*   Ruth 1:16-17

Ruth is a type of the New Covenant church, but not all of the church. Ruth was a *Gentile* and is a type of the Gentiles who by faith will be grafted as branches from a *Wild Olive Tree* into the Good Olive Tree whose (Jewish) roots are still holy. The rest of the New Covenant churches are those who like Abraham died in faith.

The Apostle Paul correctly identified how the Gentiles are heirs and joint heirs to the covenant God made with Abraham.

For as ye (Gentiles) in times past have not believed God, yet have now obtained mercy through their (Jews) unbelief: Romans 11:30

[12] *For there is no difference between the Jew and the Greek: for the same Lord over all is rich unto all that call upon him.*
[13] *For whosoever shall call upon the name of the Lord shall be saved.*   Romans 10:12-13

For if thou (Gentiles) *were cut out of the olive tree which is wild by nature, and were grafted contrary to nature into a* **good** *olive tree: how much more shall these* (Jews*), which be the natural branches, be grafted* (back) *into their own olive tree?*   Romans 11:24

Traditionally, Ruth has been seen as a type of all of the New Covenant *church*. Since Ruth is a Gentile, this would not include the Jews who by faith are saved also. This viewpoint is a classic example of those who espouse what is called *Replacement Theology*; a theological position that says since the birth of Christ the Gentiles have replaced the Jews. This belief cannot be supported Scripturally. Replacement theologians fail to recognize that the church is actually the *ecclesia* or the chosen ones composed of both Jews and Gentiles. In God's eyes, the entire world is now composed of only two groups of people, living or dead: the *ecclesia,* and the unbelievers. Ruth is only a type of the *Gentiles* who have been saved by placing their faith in the Lord Jesus Christ. In the same manner, the *Messianic Jews* are those who have been saved by the same faith and are also part of the church.

The astute reader may have asked the following question: *How could Ruth, a Moabite Gentile, embrace the Jewish faith and marry Boaz who was an Israelite?*

A Gentile woman or a Gentile man could become a Jew under the Law of Moses. It was not disallowed, but because Jews then and today protected their holy status it was generally discouraged. A male convert to Judaism is referred to by the Hebrew word *ger* (Hebrew: גֵּר, plural *gerim*) and a female convert is a *giyoret*. Both words are related to the term *proselyte*, which is a Gentile living in Israel who has converted to Judaism. In the ancient past Rabbis often rejected potential converts three times, and if they remained adamant in their desire to become part of the Jewish faith, they would then be allowed to begin the process. We see this ancient practice in the Book of Ruth. Naomi tried to get Ruth to go back to her own people *three times* before Naomi agreed to take her to Bethlehem. Recall that the story of Ruth begins in the time of the Judges. At that time, there was a great famine in the land

and Elimelech left his land with all of his family and went to the Land of Moab. God had given his family the land he left, and it was never intended to be transferred to anyone else. Whether any Jewish male *leased* the land to someone else or *sold* the land is not the issue. All land cannot be permanently sold; it always reverted back to the original landowner during every *Year of Jubilee*.

Boaz *(Strength)*

We now come to Boaz. Almost all commentators identify Boaz as the *kinsman redeemer* who is a type of *Christ*. There is much appeal to this assertion, but it is believed that this is not the prophetic picture actually projected in the Book of Ruth. In order to properly identify Boaz as a type, we must remove all preconceived notions and ask the following question: *What if Boaz is not a type of Jesus Christ? If not, who would he best represent?* In order to answer this question, we must collectively consider the true story of Ruth and Boaz as revealed in the Holy Scriptures. The story of how Boaz met and married Ruth is rooted in the Leverite Law previously discussed. Clearly, Naomi and the ancestral property of her deceased husband Elimelech were *not* redeemed by Boaz. There is something more to the story which is hidden in what actually took place. To recognize who Boaz actually represented in type, we must determine who the *nearest kinsman* was in the story of Ruth. Was it Boaz? ...... No. Recall that the *nearest* kinsman was stopped at the city gate by Boaz who confronted him with his obligation to redeem Naomi and her land, marry Ruth, sire a son, and adopt Naomi into his household. Confronted with this serious obligation, the (unnamed) nearest of kin refused to accept all of these obligations. Actually, note carefully what he said to Boaz.

[3] *And he said unto the kinsman, Naomi, that is come again out of the country of Moab, selleth a parcel of land, which was our brother Elimelech's:*

[4] *And I thought to advertise thee, saying, Buy it before the inhabitants, and before the elders of my people. If thou wilt redeem it, redeem it: but if thou wilt not redeem it, then tell me, that I may know: for there is none to redeem it beside thee; and I am after thee. And he said, I will redeem it.*

[5] *Then said Boaz, What day thou buyest the field of the hand of Naomi, thou must buy it also of Ruth the Moabitess, the wife of the dead, to raise up the name of the dead upon his inheritance.*

[6] *And the kinsman said, I* **cannot** *redeem it for myself, lest I mar mine own inheritance: redeem thou my right to thyself; for I* **cannot** *redeem it.*   Ruth 3:4-6

Note carefully that the nearest kinsman did not say that he **would not** do these things he said he **cannot** do these things. What a strange thing to say? Because he *could not* redeem Naomi and take Ruth as his bride, the Leverite Law of redemption passed down to Boaz, who was not only ready but willing to risk all he had to redeem Ruth, who was a Gentile from Moab! Boaz is often called the *kinsman redeemer,* but this is not quite correct in this strange turn of events. Boaz agreed to: (1) purchase the land of Elimelech, (2) take Ruth as his wife, (3) Adopt Naomi into his family, and (4) love and protect both Naomi and Ruth. Now please note that even if Boaz does all of this, the land and holdings of Elimelech would *not* pass into Naomi's lineage. This can *only happen* if Boaz not only marries Ruth but sires a SON to carry on the family line of the deceased Elimelech. Subsequently, we are told that although Boaz is well advanced in age, he does just that. He has a son with Ruth called *Obed.* Have you been following this logic? Have you gleaned some prophetic truth from this strange sequence of events? We will now propose that the prophetic structure of Ruth unfolds as follows.

By carefully examining the redemption story in Ruth, it must be recognized that Ruth is not the one being redeemed. *Naomi* is the one who needs restoration and redemption. The issue is one of inheritance of family land and family redemption. Ruth became involved when she married the oldest son of Naomi. We know that Mahlon was the oldest son who married Ruth because the Law of Inheritance passed family holdings on to the eldest son. From there, the son of the oldest son was next in line. This you may recall was the real problem. It was not only that Ruth was a Moabite; the real problem was that she had no son. The Leverite Law required that the kinsman redeemer give his oldest son by marriage to the afflicted family (Naomi and Ruth) to carry on the family inheritance. It now becomes clear that Boaz *and* Ruth had no sons, because Boaz had to marry Ruth and sire a son.

Moreover Ruth the Moabitess, the wife of Mahlon, have I purchased to be my wife, to raise up the name of the dead upon his inheritance, that the name of the dead be not cut off from among his brethren, and from the gate of his place: ye are witnesses this day.   Ruth 4:10

This is the path to redeem Naomi (a Jew) through Ruth (a Gentile). Do you see the type being revealed? Boaz had to give his only son (Obed) birthed by him and Ruth (Gentile) to redeem *both* Naomi (Jew) and Ruth! This is the key to properly identifying types. Boaz is a type of *God the Father* who offered His only Son Jesus Christ (a Jew) to the Gentiles, so that through the sinless life of Christ under the law He could redeem not only the *Gentiles* but also those *Jews* who lived under the Law of Moses. Those of Abraham's faith were dead under the works of the Law, but are now alive by *faith* in the coming Messiah. Those who were alienated from the promises to Abraham can now also be saved by the same faith as that of Abraham.

[4] *But when the fullness of the time was come, God sent forth his Son, made of a woman, made under the law,*
[5] **To redeem them that were under the law**, *that we might receive the adoption of sons.*   Galatians 4:4-5

It is natural to question this interpretation of type by asking the following question: *Was not Boaz called the kinsman redeemer?* He certainly was, but one must understand the role of Boaz as a type of God, Obed his son as a type of Christ and the actual kinsman redeemer.

> *The marriage of Ruth to Boaz is actually a type of the Gentiles being grafted into the commonwealth of Israel so that the Gentiles could partake of the goodness of God the father.*

This may seem strange to modern-day Christians, but the Apostle Paul made this quite clear.

[11] *Wherefore remember, that ye being in time past Gentiles in the flesh, who are called uncircumcision by that which is called the circumcision in the flesh made by hands;*
[12] *That at that time ye were without Christ, being aliens from the commonwealth of Israel, and strangers from the covenants of promise, having no hope, and without God in the world:*
[13] *But now in Christ Jesus ye who sometimes were far off are made nigh by the blood of Christ.*
[14] *For he is our peace, who hath made both one, and hath broken down the middle wall of partition between us;*
[15] *Having abolished in his flesh the enmity, even the law of commandments contained in ordinances; for to make in himself of twain one new man, so making peace;*
[16] *And that he might reconcile both unto God in one body by the cross, having slain the enmity thereby:*

Ephesians 2:11-16

Paul called this a *mystery* not revealed in the Old Testament but revealed to him personally by Jesus Christ. So, Boaz was definitely a part (initiator) of the redemptive process, but he was not the *actual* kinsman redeemer; his son Boaz was the one by which the Land of Elimelech was restored to Ruth and her family, including Naomi. *Boaz is not a type of Jesus Christ. He is a type of God the father.* He was the *origin* of redemption and Obed is the *agent* of redemption.

It is clear that Boaz is a kinsman redeemer in the Book of Ruth, but he is not the closest kinsman redeemer. *What price did Boaz pay to redeem Naomi?* It is true that Boaz opened up his home to Ruth and Naomi, and that he redeemed (bought back) the ancestral land of Elimelech, but he did not sacrifice the life of his only son to redeem Naomi (Israel). It was Obed who was able to redeem not only Naomi (Israel) but also Ruth (Gentile). It is well-understood that Christ Jesus paid the ultimate price for our sins, but what is often not recognized is the price that God the Father paid to save not only faithful Israel but faithful Gentiles. How would you like to send your only begotten son into the world knowing the pain and misery that He would suffer on the Day of Pentecost? Who could stand by and not intervene when his son cried out to him: *My God, My God, why have you forsaken me?* Such pain and sorrow is unspeakable. However, the next words of Christ were: Nevertheless, *not my will but thy will be done.* Christ came to redeem all mankind not only because he loved us and chose to do so, but because the Father had planned this before time began. God the father was never to actually execute redemption on the cross; his only Son was destined to do that. Christ said that he was obedient in every way, and that He did not say or do anything unless the Father told Him to do it. God (Boaz) was the *origin* of redemption and Christ (Obed) was the *agent* of redemption. It was by and through Jesus Christ that both Jews and Gentiles are justified, glorified, and sanctified, but Christ was the one through which redemption flowed. God the Father was the one who planned and ordained redemption. When the fullness of the time was come, God sent forth his Son, made of a woman, made under the law:

To redeem them that were under the law, that we might receive the adoption of sons.   Galatians 4:5

Abraham's covenant was based on faith and we are heirs of his promises or the unconditional covenant with God.

Now we, brethren, as Isaac was, are the children of promise.   Galatians 4:28.

The *new covenant* was promised to the Jews, not to the Gentiles! The Gentiles were heirs to the promises God made long ago to Abraham and it was confirmed to Jeremiah the prophet long ago.

[31] *Behold, the days come, saith the LORD, that I will make a **new covenant** with the house of Israel, **and** with the house of Judah:*
[32] *Not according to the covenant that I made with their fathers in the day that I took them by the hand to bring them out of the land of Egypt; which my covenant they broke, although I was an husband unto them, saith the LORD:*
[33] *But this shall be the **covenant** that I will make with the house of Israel; After those days, saith the LORD, I will put my law in their inward parts, and write it in their hearts; and will be their God, and they shall be my people.*
Jeremiah 31:31-33

The new covenant was initiated by the sacrificial death of Jesus Christ. The old covenant had passed away, and the new covenant had arrived. The law was added to the old covenant through Moses because of the disobedience and faithlessness of the Children of Israel. It was initiated to show Israel that they could not gain salvation by works under the Laws of Moses, but redemption could only come through a promised redeemer and Messiah, Jesus Christ the Son of God. This fully explains what the Apostle Paul revealed to us in Galatians.

[3] *Know ye therefore that they which are of faith, the same are the children of Abraham.*
[8] *And the scripture, foreseeing that God would justify the heathen through faith, preached before the gospel unto Abraham, saying: In thee shall all nations be blessed.*
[9] *So then **they which are of faith** are blessed with faithful Abraham.*   Galatians 3:7-9

The law could not alter or annul the Abrahamic promises that God had made. Rather, the law was only temporary until Christ, *the Seed*, came as the Son of Man and the Son of God. The Law was a *schoolmaster* to bring Israel into the realization that a redeemer was coming who would take away their transgressions and sins,

Wherefore then serveth the law? It was added because of transgressions, till the seed should come to whom the promise was made   Galatians 3:19

Now that faith has come, we are no longer under the supervision of the law   Galatians 3:19

[24] *Wherefore **the law was our schoolmaster** to bring us unto Christ, that we might be justified by faith.*
[25] *But after that faith is come, we are no longer under a schoolmaster.*
[26] *For ye are all the children of God by faith in Christ Jesus.*
[27] *For as many of you as have been baptized into Christ have put on Christ.*
[28] *There is neither Jew nor Greek, there is neither bond nor free, there is neither male nor female: for ye are all one*

in Christ Jesus.
[29] *And if ye be Christ's, then are ye* (Gentiles*)*
***Abraham's seed**, and heirs according to the promise.*
Galations3:24-29

It should now be understood that Boaz is not a type of Jesus
Christ but of God the Father. So who is the type of Jesus
Christ?

Obed (*Servant* or *To Serve*)

There is one person in the story of Ruth that is usually just
mentioned and dismissed as simply part of the story. That
person is *Obed* who was the *son* born to *Boaz and Ruth.* In
reality, the son is the object and fulfillment of the whole
story. The tragedy that befell Naomi was that her husband
and two sons had died in Moab leaving her destitute. The
real problem was that there was no male heir to perpetuate
the land and house of Elimelech! The one who fulfilled the
role of a kinsman redeemer *had* to sire a son with Ruth to
fulfill this role. As already discussed, Boaz was well-
advanced in age, and was not expecting to sire any more
children. This reminds us of Abram and Sarai, who were
not blessed with a sibling until both were well past child-
bearing age. It is interesting that Abram and Sarai both
grew old nearing 100 years. Sarai was well aware of the
covenant that God had made with Abraham that out of his
loins would arise many nations and that his seed (singular)
would give rise to a Messiah that would take away the sins
of Israel, all who would believe in that covenant promise.
Sarai decided to take things in her own hands. She offered
her handmaiden Hagar to sleep with Abram and father a
son. Abram had a son called *Ishmael.* This was a terrible
act of unbelief, but God had made an unconditional
covenant with Abram. He met with Sarah and Abram when
Abram was 99 years old   and Sarah was 89 years old
(Genesis 17:17, 17:1)). God changed Abram's name to
Abraham and Sari's name to Sarah; Sarah immediately

became pregnant and at age 90 gave birth to the child of promise, and named him *Issac*. Since Ishmael was a child of rebellion and disbelief, the Messiah Jesus Christ came out of the line of Issac (Matthew 1:1-16). In God, all things are possible!

Obed was the *son* of aging Boaz and Ruth. Obed is the male offspring who was the object of redemption for Naomi and Ruth. *He is in every way a type of Jesus Christ.*

The Nearest Kinsman Redeemer

The nearest kinsman redeemer is unnamed. The nearest kinsman redeemer is somewhat of a mystery. Two times the unnamed kinsman redeemer said he *cannot* redeem Ruth. We have shown that *Boaz* and *Obed* are types of *God the Father* and *God the Son*, respectively. So who is the unnamed nearest redeemer? We suggest that the (unnamed) nearest kinsman redeemer is a type of the *Holy Spirit*. The Holy Spirit is never characterized or involved in the redemptive process. The ministry of the Holy Spirit is to bear witness of Jesus (John 15:26). Jesus told His apostles:

I will ask the Father, and He will give you another Helper, that He may be with you forever; the Spirit of truth, whom the world cannot receive, because it does not behold Him or know Him, but you know Him because He abides with you, and will be in you. I will not leave you as orphans; I will come to you.   John 14:16-18

All the divine attributes ascribed to the Father and the Son are equally ascribed to the Holy Spirit. This is what Christians call the *Holy Trinity*. When a person becomes born again by believing and receiving Jesus Christ (John 1:12-13; John 3:3-21), God resides in that person through the Holy Spirit (1Cor. 3:16). The Holy Spirit is not *directly* involved in the redemptive work of Jesus Christ, but is not completely outside of that wonderful process. The Holy Spirit was not given to *all* believers (Jews and Gentiles) before Jesus Christ ascended into heaven, but was given to some. A primary role of the Holy Spirit is that He bears *witness* of Jesus Christ (John 15:26, 16:14). He tells people's hearts about the truth of Jesus Christ, and helps to discern the word of God (I Cor. 2:9-14). He reveals God's will and God's truth to every true believer, Jew or Gentile. Was Paul not a Jew? Was Peter not a Jew?

[7] *Nevertheless I tell you the truth; It is expedient for you that I go away: for if I go not away, the Comforter will not come unto you; but if I depart, I will send him unto you.*
 [8] *And when he is come, he will convict the world of sin, and of righteousness, and of judgment of sin*
because they believe not on me;   John 16:7-9

The unnamed nearest kinsman in the Book of Ruth *cannot* redeem Naomi and Ruth because it is not his primary role in God's eternal plan of salvation. The covenant promise to Abraham was explained not only by Paul but by Peter.

*Who verily was foreordained before the **foundation** of the world, but was manifest in these last times for you*
I Peter 1:20

Now to Abraham and his seed were the promises made. He saith not, and to seeds, as of many; but as of one, and to thy seed, which is Christ.   Galatians 3:16

The eternal plan of God was to redeem all mankind through His Son Jesus Christ. God cannot lie and His covenant promise to Abraham was unconditional. It is reasonable to assume that the nearest kinsman redeemer was part of the redemptive process, but he was neither the *origin* nor the

130

agent of redemption. The nearest kinsman in the Book of Ruth is a type of the *Holy Spirit*.

In summary, The Book of Ruth is remarkable in both its content and structure. It is categorized as a book of history and as part of the *writings (Ketuvim)* in the Christian canon. In light of revealed prophecy, it should take its rightful place among the great books of prophetic revelation in the Holy Scriptures. The Book of Ruth is an Old Testament bookend to the New Testament Book of Romans. As New Testament Christians, we might also ask:

Who is the Bride of Christ?

In the New Testament, we are told that the *Church* will be the Bride of Christ. But, do you realize that God already had a bride in the Old Testament?

*Return, O backsliding children," says the Lord; "for **I am married to you**. I will take you, one from a city and two from a family, and I will bring you to Zion.* Jeremiah 3:14

*Behold, the days are coming, says the Lord, when I will make a new covenant with the house of Israel and with the house of Judah - not according to the covenant that I made with their fathers in the day that I took them by the hand to lead them out of the land of Egypt, My covenant which they broke, though **I was a husband to them**, says the Lord. But this is the covenant that I will make with the house of Israel after those days, says the Lord: I will put My law in their minds, and write it on their hearts; and I will be their God, and they shall be My people.* Jeremiah 31:31-33

It may be a mystery to most modern-day Christians, but the Bride of Christ is not the same as the Bride of Jehovah God. Although both represent believers who were bought with a price and redeemed from sin, they are not the same group. Israel, the apple of God's eye, has been unfaithful to her Husband; but as unfaithful as Israel has been, God promises to stand by her. God will yet have a bride of Old Testament saints who believed in His promises to send a kinsman redeemer (Christ His Son).

It can now be further understood why the nearest kinsman redeemer probably could not redeem Ruth. If he was already married he might have wished to remain faithful to one bride (Israel). Boaz (Jesus Christ) loved Ruth (Gentile) and Naomi (Israel) so much that he was willing to give himself and his inherited possessions to redeem *both* Ruth and Naomi (Jews and Gentiles). How *perfect* is this a shadow and type of Jesus Christ who gave all He had to redeem both Gentiles and Jews to redeem all sinners and reconcile them to His Father. Recall and understand that in the current disposition of grace that there are only two different types of people in the Ecclesia regardless of color, nationality or religion. This body is composed of all those believers who died before Christ came (Old Testament saints) and all those believers who died after Christ came (New Testament saints). The *New Testament saints* will be the *Bride of Christ* and the *Old Testament saints* will be the *Bride of Jehovah God.* When Christ is married to His bride after the Battle of Armageddon, the Old Testament saints will be the *Wedding Guests*, since they are already taken as a bride.

Who Are The Wedding Guests?

In Jeremiah 31:31-33, God says that His covenant was confirmed by a marriage to the people of natural Israel. God is said to be their husband, and those Jews of faith will be His wife. This is an Old Covenant pattern for the New

Covenant. One marriage was to a natural people (New Testament believers) who accept Christ as their savior, and the other to a spiritual people (Old Testament believers).

We admit that the term *Bride of Christ* never explicitly appears in the New Testament, but the marriage of the Lamb to His bride will definitely take place following the resurrection and rapture of all saints.

[7] *Let us be glad and rejoice, and give honour to him: for the marriage of the Lamb is come, and his wife hath made herself ready.*
[8] *And to her was granted that she should be arrayed in fine linen, clean and white: for the fine linen is the righteousness of saints.* Revelation 19:7-8

It is interesting to now reveal a *mystery* of God. In Revelation 19, following the pouring out of the 7th bowl judgment, in Revelation 19:7-8 we are told that the Marriage of the Lamb is come, but in Revelation 19:8 there is a larger group mentioned at the wedding who are in attendance.

*And he saith unto me, Write, Blessed are they which are **called** unto the marriage supper of the Lamb.*
Revelation 19: 9

The bride is never called to a wedding; only wedding guests are called or invited. *Who are the blessed that are called to the wedding ceremony of the Lamb?* (Revelation 19:7-9). Surely the bride is blessed to join Christ in marriage, but the wedding guests are possibly more blessed. The New Testament Saints all died (or were raptured alive) knowing by faith that they would be resurrected from the dead just as Christ was resurrected from the dead. In fact, Christ said that the only sign that He would give that He was the Son of God would be the sign of Noah, that He would spend 3 days and 3 nights in the grave and then rise. The Old Testament saints all died in faith, and believed not only in a Messiah who would yet appear but in who they knew very little about; the New Testament scriptures had not been written. The *Bride* of Christ is composed of all New Covenant saints. The *Body of Christ* is all New Covenant believers who are functioning as Jesus Christ and His disciples to proclaim the gospel message to all unbelievers. At the end of their days, they will join the other New Covenant believers who have died in Christ. But there is another group of saints who will join the New Covenant believers to form the *ecclesia* or the *chosen ones*. This is the New Covenant Jewish believers who have died in faith, believing that Jesus Christ was the promised Messiah. The scriptures make it clear that the Body of Christ, the New Covenant believers, will be the Bride of Christ. As just discussed, it might come as a surprise to many born-again Christians that God has already taken a bride in the Old Testament. This bride is the Old Covenant patriarchs and God fearing Children of Israel that died believing in faith that they would be redeemed and their sins forgiven by a coming Messiah.

All Old Testament saints, just like the New Testament saints were saved by *faith*. When God chose Israel as His chosen people, He also took the Nation of Israel as His bride.

*Turn, O backsliding children, saith the LORD; for **I am married unto you**: and I will take you one of a city, and two of a family, and I will bring you to Zion* (after the Tribulation Period and the Rapture)

Jeremiah 2:14

Jeremiah states in no uncertain terms that God will be married to the Children of Israel. However, the bride whom God chose was unfaithful. When they finally recognize Christ as their Messiah, they will return as His bride.

But you have played the harlot with many lovers; yet return to Me," says the Lord.   Jeremiah 3:1

Jesus Christ, the risen Son of God will be married to the New Testament believers. However, a believing remnant of Israel (Jews) will be saved by Jesus Christ just as the Gentiles are under the New Covenant. The New Testament Gentile believers will be grafted into the Good Olive Tree, and the Jewish men and women of faith who were broken off will be grafted back into the tree. The Bible says that Israel is being provoked to *jealousy* (Rom 10:19). *What is the nature of jealousy*? Jealousy occurs when someone has something that you desire, or has something you own that you thought was only yours. This was exactly what Paul was dealing with in both his letter to the Romans and the letter to the Hebrews. The Jews could not believe that they being the chosen people would now have to share their chosen status with the Gentiles! The Gentiles had been grafted into the previously exclusive tree of commonwealth Israel Jewish believers through the life and sacrificial death of Jesus Christ, and they were jealous! In reality, both Jews and Gentiles share a better covenant with God through His son Jesus Christ because the Law no longer keeps a person in bondage.

I will call them my people, which were not my people; and her beloved, which was not beloved.   Romans 9:25

God is longsuffering and merciful, and even though His bride committed adultery with other gods, He will yet forgive her and once again embrace her as His bride.

In Hosea 2, Hosea is told to marry a harlot, so that he will know how it feels for God to have to constantly chastise and forgive His bride. God then directly relates that unfaithful bride to Israel, and vows that He will yet bring His bride back by grace. In Hosea 2:16, it says:

In that day, declares the Lord, **you will call me my husband;** *you will no longer call me my master* Hos. 2:16

Then in Hosea 2:19-20:

I will betroth you to Me forever; *I will betroth you in righteousness and justice, in love and compassion. I will betroth you in faithfulness, and you will acknowledge the Lord.* Hosea 2:19-20

These passages confirm that the Children of Israel were taken as the Bride of God, but they apostatized and committed adultery with other gods so God temporarily set them aside. However, in His mercy, He will once again claim them as His eternal bride. Note that the bride of Christ and the Bride of God can only take their place in one way, by believing in the Lord Jesus Christ as their redeemer and savior. In the Old Testament, Christ was the *Messiah of Promise* and in the New Testament that promise was made a reality.

It is natural to again ask the following question: If Christ is to marry the church as His bride following the rapture of the Saints who remain alive after the great tribulation and the Resurrection of all the dead in Christ (Old and New Testament saints), how can the Old Testament believers be both the Bride of Jehovah and of Christ? The answer is clear, they cannot. The resolution of this issue solves a great *mystery*. Christ affirmed that He was the bridegroom, but did not explicitly define his bride.

*And Jesus said unto them, Can the children of the bride chamber mourn, as long as the **bridegroom** is with them? but the days will come, when the **bridegroom** shall be taken from them, and then shall they fast.*   Matthew 9:15

*But the days will come, when the **bridegroom** shall be taken away from them, and then shall they fast in those days.*
Luke 5:35

The Old Testament saints will be a part of redeemed sinners, but they will not be a part of the Bride of Christ. *Then who are they at the wedding ceremony?* They are the wedding guests!

The wedding guests are those original branches from the Old Tree who once were alienated from God, but by faith were counted as righteous; Just as Abraham's faith was counted to him as righteousness.

[7] *Know ye therefore that they which are of faith, the same are the children of **Abraham**.*
[8] *And the scripture, foreseeing that God would justify the heathen through faith, preached before the gospel unto **Abraham**, saying, In thee shall all nations be blessed.*
[9] *So then they which are of faith are blessed with faithful **Abraham**.*
[14] *That the blessing of **Abraham** might come on the Gentiles through Jesus Christ; that we might receive the promise of the Spirit through faith.*   Galatians 3:7-9, 14

This conjecture is made almost certain by the following statement made by John the Baptizer,

*He that hath the bride is the **bridegroom**: but the **friend of the bridegroom**, which standeth and heareth him, rejoiceth greatly because of the **bridegroom**'s voice: this my joy therefore is fulfilled.*   John 3:29

137

John the Baptizer lived under the Law of Moses and died under the Old Covenant. He had the rare privilege of seeing the promised Messiah with his own eyes but he was saved by *faith*, just as was every other Jew or Gentile. Nevertheless, he was part of the Old Testament saints. He knew that he would not be part of the Bride of Christ, but he was sure that he would be a *friend of the Bridegroom* or a Wedding Guest.

The Parable of the Wise and Foolish Virgins

We will not go through an exegesis of the *Parable of the Wise and Foolish Virgins* in Matthew 25, but it can now be determined that this parable has nothing whatsoever to do with the rapture of believers. Almost universally misunderstood, it is describing the *Wedding Guests.* The church (bride of Christ) is nowhere even hinted in this parable; it deals with the Nation of Israel *before* the redeeming work of Christ on the cross of Calvary. The *wise virgins* have made themselves ready to attend the marriage of the lamb by clothing themselves in the Grace and Righteousness of Jesus Christ by faith as prophesied by all of the Old Testament prophets. The *foolish virgins* are those Old Testament Children of Israel who refused to believe the promise of a Messiah (Jesus Christ) who would redeem them and pay for their sins. They all died in disbelief under the curse of the law. They all had *oil* in their lamps (the Law of Moses), but the Old Testament saints had run out of oil; when Jesus Christ their Messiah was crucified they failed to accept Him as the long awaited Messiah who would not only take away their sins but would take away the sins of the entire world… past and future, Jews and Gentiles alike. Other Jews (including Abraham, Noah and all the Jewish patriarchs) did not see Jesus Christ, but believed He was coming. Jesus Christ was not the *nearest* kinsman redeemer of the Jews, God was.

The kinsman redeemer Jesus Christ is worthy to be praised because He took away all of the sins of the world, Jews and Gentiles alike. The Old Testament Jews who believed upon Him by faith as their long-awaited redeemer are those virgins who believed in the promises. They would be resurrected from the dead (dry bones) with all the other New Testament saints (the dry bones), along with all of the Jews who accept Christ as their redeemer under the New Covenant. They were the branches that were *grafted back into the good olive tree*. The Gentile believers (the wild olive branches) were also *grafted into the good tree* and were heirs and joint heirs of the promises of God. *He who has an ear to hear, Let them understand.*

Summary and Conclusions

The following diagrams depict the prophetic structure of the Book of Ruth and how it relates to the Good Tree of the apostle Paul in Romans 11.

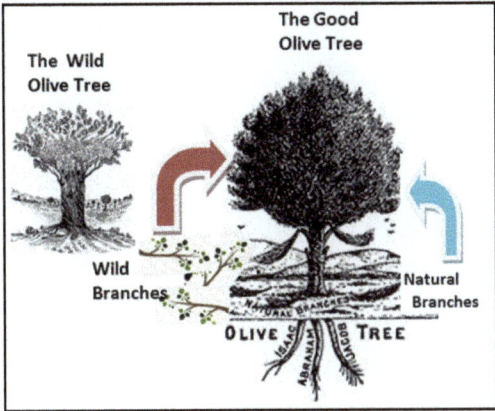

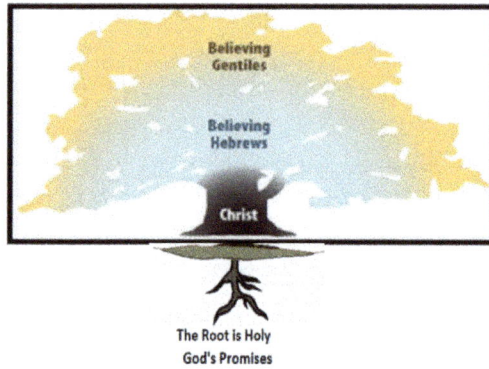

The Root is Holy
God's Promises

- God planted the good olive tree (Israel)
- The Children of Israel were the original branches
- Because of unbelief, some of the branches were *broken off* (Elimelech, Naomi, Chilion, and Mahlon)
- Some of the original branches remained, and grew strong in faith (Abraham and his faithful seed).
- Ruth and Orpah (Gentiles) married Chilion and Mahlon (Jews)
- Elimelech, Mahlon, and Chilion all died in Moab (sin). Their branches withered and died and were not grafted back into the tree (Abrahams unfaithful seed)
- Naomi, Ruth and Orpah set out to return to Bethlehem. Orpah turns back to Moab (Dies in Sin).
- Naomi and Ruth return to Israel (Naomi is grafted back into the good tree). Ruth (a Gentile and part of the Wild Olive Tree) becomes a woman of faith and is grafted into the good (natural) tree.
- The nearest kinsman redeemer *cannot* marry Ruth. He is a type of the Holy Spirit.
- The next nearest Kinsman (Boaz) marries Ruth (Gentile).

- Boaz is a type of God the Father who is the *agent* of redemption.
- Boaz has a son (Obed) who will redeem *both* Naomi (Jew) and Ruth (Gentile).
- Obed is a type of Jesus Christ who is the *instrument* of redemption.

The prophetic beauty of the Book of Ruth has been hidden throughout the ages because when this drama actually took place, Jesus Christ had not yet appeared. The *mystery* of Jesus Christ remained hidden for almost a thousand years. Most Jewish believers are still looking for the promised Messiah. Some have had the scales fall from their spiritual eyes, and have become what is now called *Jewish Christians*. This is an oxymoron since a person is either a Jew or a Christian; they cannot be both. These Jewish converts are best called *Messianic Jews*. Corporately, the Jews continue in disbelief by recognizing Christ as a prophet and a good man only. May we pray unceasingly that they will turn to Jesus Christ as their redeemer.

Amen. Let it be so.

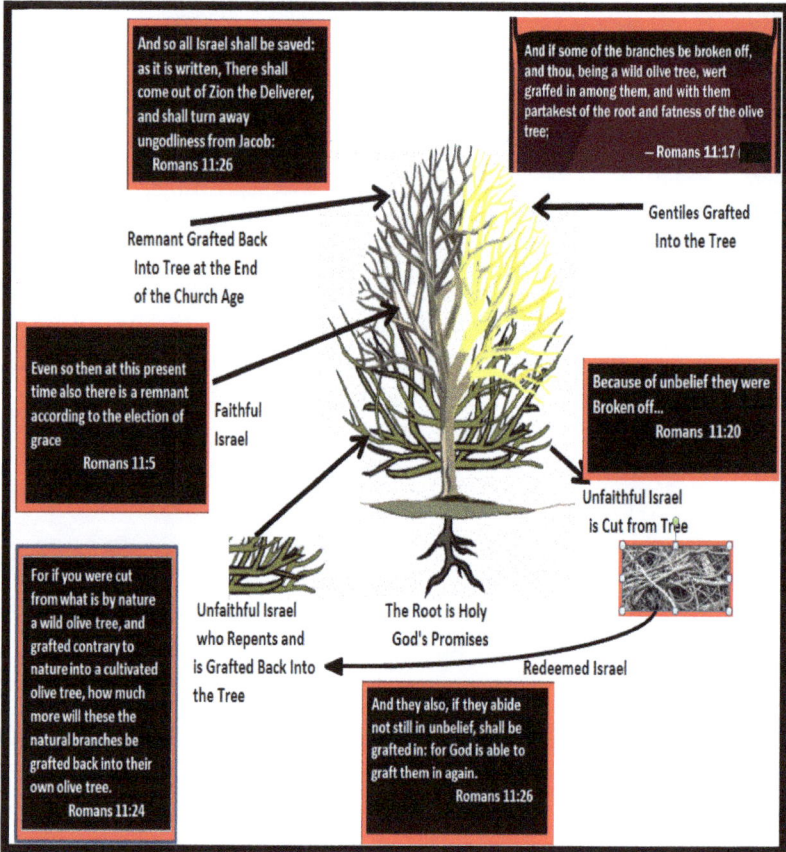

And so all Israel shall be saved: as it is written, There shall come out of Zion the Deliverer, and shall turn away ungodliness from Jacob: Romans 11:26

And if some of the branches be broken off, and thou, being a wild olive tree, wert graffed in among them, and with them partakest of the root and fatness of the olive tree; — Romans 11:17

Remnant Grafted Back Into Tree at the End of the Church Age

Gentiles Grafted Into the Tree

Even so then at this present time also there is a remnant according to the election of grace Romans 11:5

Faithful Israel

Because of unbelief they were Broken off... Romans 11:20

Unfaithful Israel is Cut from Tree

For if you were cut from what is by nature a wild olive tree, and grafted contrary to nature into a cultivated olive tree, how much more will these the natural branches be grafted back into their own olive tree. Romans 11:24

Unfaithful Israel who Repents and is Grafted Back Into the Tree

The Root is Holy God's Promises

Redeemed Israel

And they also, if they abide not still in unbelief, shall be grafted in: for God is able to graft them in again. Romans 11:26

142

References

Other Books by Don T. Phillips

The Book of Revelation: *Mysteries Revealed*

The Book of Exodus: *Historical and Prophetic Truths*

The Birth and Death of Christ

A Biblical Chronology from Adam to Christ

A Sequential Chronology of End Time Events

A Sequential Chronology of End Time Events, Expanded Edition

All are available from:

Virtual Bookworm Publishing Company, PO Box 9949, College Station Texas, 77842

www.virtualbookworm.com

www.ingramcontent.com/pod-product-compliance
Lightning Source LLC
Chambersburg PA
CBHW040418110426
42813CB00013B/2695